H.M.P

Help Me Prepare

A Guide to prison for first-timers and their families

Christopher Alston & Terry Ellis

Copyright © 2020 Terence David Ellis All rights reserved

The characters and events portrayed in this book are fictitious. Any similarity to real persons, living or dead, is coincidental and not intended by the author.

No part of this book may be reproduced, or stored in a retrieval system, or transmitted in any form or by any means, electronic, mechanical, photocopying, recording, or otherwise, without express written permission of the publisher.

ISBN-13: 9798670708111

Cover design by: Christopher Alston

Dedications

Joe Chapman

Joe became a good friend of ours after the release of Terry's first book, Living amongst the beasts.

Aside from his friendship and assistance, Joe is a former prison officer, a prison law consultant and an accomplished and talented author in his own right.

Joe has been a constant source of praise and inspiration for both of us and after 44 years of dedicated service in the criminal justice system, he continues to support ex-offenders looking to turn their lives around.

He has dedicated his life to supporting those who have fallen foul of the law and his contribution to this book not only provided us with information about a section of the prison system we knew little about, he also provided a sounding board for us to provide information to people facing a prison sentence that would also assist the officers that will be in charge of those people.

Thank you for your continued friendship, we look forward to the coming book releases from you.

Colette Goldthorpe - Nourish Wellness Sanctuary

Colette "Letti" works as a Health and Wellness coach helping people to realise their true selves and unleash their potential; her expertise was used to help us shape our advice for healthier mental and physical wellbeing whilst navigating through a prison sentence.

Colette was responsible for keeping Chris sane during the 2020 coronavirus pandemic and a cherished friend of well over 10 years.

Despite being separated by nearly 5000 miles we have managed to maintain a good friendship and we were delighted when you agree to contribute to the book in your specialized field of mindfulness and wellbeing.

Despite being in the process of setting up your own business you made the time available to help us to write part of the book, help with the proofreading process and we are eternally grateful and fortunate that you did.

And to top it off, you never complained once when my chaotic desk management meant that I missed some of the changes you originally sent over.

"Good friends are like stars. You don't always see them, but you know they're always there" - Christy Evans

Anna Wheatley

For your continued support, love and patience.

Books from the Author's

VERIZON - CAMDEN'S $100 MILLION HEIST:

Verizon Paperback – April 26, 2021
by Mr Terry Ellis (Author), Mr Chris Alston (Editor)
★★★★☆ ~ 10 ratings

In 2007 the Verizon business Centre, King's Cross London played host to one of the UK's most brazen and audacious heists since the great train Robbery.

Boasting one of the Worlds most sophisticated security systems and hosting some of the most valuable banking data for several of the worlds leading banks, Verizon was considered one of the toughest jobs in the criminal underworld. Located in the middle of three large London police stations it would require expert planning and nerves of steel to even contemplate entry.

Then one evening a police fast response team would descend on the building and take control. Except it wasn't a police team, it was Camden's very own "Ocean's Eleven" gang; using disguise and deception to gain control over the whole security operation they would leave without raising the alarm with data chips worth £5million and data worth £100million.

HMP GRENDON - THERAPEUTIC PRISON:

Living amongst the beasts: The rise and fall of the Grendon experiment
by Mr Terry Ellis, Mr Christopher Alston, et al. | 26 May 2020
★★★★★ ~ 141

Paperback
£10⁰⁰
Get it Monday, May 3
FREE Delivery by Amazon

Kindle Edition
£0⁰⁰
kindleunlimited
Free with Kindle Unlimited membership
Learn More
Or £7.00 to buy

HMP SPRINGHILL - RESETTLEMENT PRISON:

The Final Countdown to my Freedom: Resettlement Diaries
by Mr Terry Ellis and Mr Christopher James Alston | 1 Dec 2020
★★★★★ ~ 10

Paperback
£9⁹⁹
Get it Monday, May 3
Eligible for FREE UK Delivery

Kindle Edition
£0⁰⁰
kindleunlimited
Free with Kindle Unlimited membership
Learn More
Or £6.97 to buy

Booking the Authors

Both authors are available together for after-dinner speaking, college or university talks, motivational speaking and media work.

We can also arrange talks with a former serving prison officer, Joe Chapman and a victim of a serious violent crime, Darren Barden.

Twitter:

https://twitter.com/Sealing_Futures
https://twitter.com/TerryEllis992

Facebook:

https://www.facebook.com/TerryEllisAuthor/?ref=bookmarks

Email:

Terryellis992@gmail.com
christopher.alston@hotmail.co.uk

We welcome feedback about our work and can be contacted via the above channels.

Chapter 1 - Court 1
Getting your personal effects in order 1
Suggested kit bag 2
Holding Cells 5
Transport to prison 6

Types of prison and prisoner 10
Categorisation 10

And now you're a prisoner 13
Reception/Check-In 13
The first phone call 16
Moving to your first wing 17
The first night 18
Induction 22
First timer and at-risk wing 24
Hygiene and the complete lack of privacy 25
Vulnerable Prisoner Wing 26
Apps (not phone apps) 35
Pitfalls - What to avoid in your first few days 38

Your first proper wing - the first few weeks 41
Your first cell and cellmate 43
Bang-up **Error! Bookmark not defined.**
Regime 45
IEP - Incentives and Earned Privileges 47

Personal Officer	49
OMU (Offender Management Unit) - Sentence plan	50
Meals	51
Kit day / allocation	53
Canteen - Spends	54
Catalogue Spends	56
Contact with the outside world	56
First VO (Visiting Order)	58
Pitfalls - What to avoid	59
Work and Education	**62**
Education	63
Work	65
Learning to read	66
Distance learning - Open University	67
Occupying your time (this is something you have plenty of)	**68**
Exercise	68
Association/free time	70
Gym	71
Faith	71
Library	72
Examples of Prisoner Art	73
Information for families	**75**
Visits	75
Post	78
Sending in money	79
Leave a message	81
Research for inmates	82

Help with visits	*83*
Vulnerable Prisoners - Family Support	*86*

Support in Prison — 101

Healthcare	*101*
Listeners	*102*
Reps - violence reduction	*104*
Prison discipline system	*105*
Complaints procedure	*109*

Progressing with your sentence — 111

Alternative therapies	*111*
Mindfulness	*113*
Mindful Movement	*119*
Yoga	*121*
Health and Nutrition	*124*
Final Thought	*127*
Drug and Alcohol programs	*128*
Vulnerable Prisoners - This is your life - The OASYS	*130*
Vulnerable Prisoners - The Kaizen Course	*136*
Transfers	*142*
"Resettlement" jails	*144*
Probation	*147*
Terry's favourite topic - CRC's	*148*
ROTL (Release on Temporary License)	*154*
Relationships on release	*155*

Our opinion of the Justice system — 156

Courts and Legal Aid	*159*
Drug de-criminalisation - Time for a conversation?	*162*

The prison system 164

Final Thought 171

Useful Links 173

Preface

The goal of us writing this book was never just about producing a mundane prison procedure handbook that lacked personality.

We didn't want to glorify or horrify prison in any way, what we wanted to do was given an honest account of the prison system using the first-hand experience.

The book will appeal to anyone with an interest in how UK prisons operate but our specific aim was to dispel myths about prisons for people facing their first sentence and their families because it is hard to find out information about what happens and the process you will go through.

We also offer our thoughts on what doesn't work within the justice system and what we would change.

Many countries around the world use ex-inmates to inform and influence how their justice system works yet this country is reluctant to do so.

A properly functioning justice system reduces reoffending, encourages and helps offenders to turn around their lives. However, the people that currently decide what works and what doesn't, have never lived through the system so how could they possibly know how to change it.

Throughout this book, we offer advice on what to avoid and how to make better-informed decisions for inmates in order for you to get the most out of your sentence.

Foreword

Over the past 50 years, there have been books written about prisons, by academics, former prison Governors, Ex-prison officers and ex-prisoners, at an ever-increasing rate, and they all make a valuable contribution to the public's understanding of Crime and Punishment in the UK.

It took Terry Ellis four years to produce his first book, originally entitled *"Living Amongst the Beasts"* which is the story of his journey through therapy at HMP Grendon. The rather controversial title was later changed to *"Grendon's Therapy – The Inside Story"*, to appeal to the more sensitive audience, although the content remains the same, and he opens up an interesting debate about the process of prison therapy, particularly mixing sex offenders with mainstream prisoners.

Having witnessed its success, and realising that there was a need for a further book, that would help people to prepare themselves for going to prison, he has written *"Help Me Prepare"*, which is an easier accessible guide for those finding themselves at the mercy of our courts. One that is written in a style that will appeal to the average reader, that is useful to prisoners' families, and that will inform the general public in a way that other books have not done.

Terry Ellis is a reformed armed robber, not just respected by those in the criminal fraternity that he used to associate with, many of whom have reformed themselves, but also by the people who have witnessed his tireless journey towards redemption. If he could turn the clock back on his life, then I am sure there would be many things he would change and certainly fewer victims.

But this book is not about self-promotion, which many are, it is about pulling together all of the experience and knowledge he has gained over the years, to help others through their journey.

It is the case that nobody can write about prison life unless they have experienced it themselves, nobody can promote change unless they have changed, and the most important thing missing in libraries across the UK, and prison libraries is a book that will be of immediate help to prisoners and their families, right from the beginning.

At the moment we are swamped with information online. There has never been a time when people can access so much about the Police procedures, Criminal Justice System, Sentencing Frameworks, Prison Service Instructions, Public Protection policies and Probation Service Supervision. However, for many families, and particularly those who struggle with technology, there is nothing better than being able to flick through easy to read pages, which are produced in a language that will not confuse.

Here is a book that can be given to men and women, at a time when they need it most, which answers questions directly, without jargon, sometimes light-hearted but with a serious intention. In the fast-moving world of Prisons, there is often no time to contemplate the information received before another piece comes along. *"Help Me Prepare"* takes it all down a gear and provides just the right amount of information to survive.

Joe Chapman - Former 'award winning' Prison Officer, Prison Law Consultant and Author.

Introduction
Covid-19 Update

Prisons have not been immune from the global pandemic and no matter what your feelings are about prisoner welfare the simple fact is that they have been forgotten by the UK Government.

Regimes were moved to 23 hour "bang-up" early on in the pandemic and they have never returned to date (June 2021).

For many, visits are still not happening and the impact of that is seen in an increase in phone use but no increase in the amount of time allocated to using the phones, so you end up with a full wing trying to use 2 to 4 phones at every unlock.

Friends and family are often what keep inmates going, therefore we encourage you to write as much as possible, even if you have nothing much to say; the contact will mean so much to your loved one and is likely to keep them going.

Covid has not been easy for anyone but it has been especially harsh on prisoners.

So, you, or someone you know is about to be sent to prison. It's a worrying time, the unknown is always a cause of fear.

The purpose of this book is not to glorify prison, no doubt you have heard stories about prison being easy and days spent playing games consoles and pool.

Whilst there will be elements of the stories you have heard about prison being true, a large amount will be fantasy, told by men who wish to hide the real story of their time and make out that they were in a holiday camp.

Our goal is to inform you, we will give you a firsthand account of our extensive knowledge of the prison system which includes over 16 years of lived experience within the system, at some of the UK's toughest jails.

We have also spoken to hundreds of former inmates and their families with the sole aim of being a source of helpful information.

During his time in a resettlement prison, Terry was padded up with a senior prisoner called Bob who was doing his first prison sentence. Bob asked him a series of questions that, on the surface, seemed self-explanatory for someone that been in prison but to Bob, it was a minefield of uncertainties, not only for him but for his family.

This was the catalyst for us deciding to write this book HMP - Help Me Prepare, a guide to prison for first-timers and their families, as there was a huge gap in the market because there wasn't anything easily accessible for first-time offenders or their families.

The only information we were able to find were books of PSI's, rules and regulations written by people who, it seemed had little or no idea of what it is like in the first few weeks from an inmate's perspective and the obstacles that you have to overcome during those first few days, weeks and months and it starts the second you hear those immortal words "You're Guilty" by the presiding judge.

Alternatively hearing that you are to be held on remand will be the start of the journey that is your new world within a world, where you become a number and not a human being, where normal rules of society become a blur and are replaced with a set of different laws and procedures that you have to live by, as failure to adhere will see you placed on an IEP (page 47) or put down the block for good order and discipline, a contradiction in terms but a charge you will get used to, as it's now your new life.

After hearing those words "you're guilty", the minutes and hours that follow will be a haze, nothing that is said after hearing those words will be properly processed. The cold handcuffs will be slapped on, then the severity of the words you have just heard will slowly sink in.

As you are led down to the holding cells (the phrase "being sent down" originates from this moment) you will quickly be trying to work out your release date and when you will be reunited with your friends, family and loved ones again.

Remember, prison doesn't have to be the end of your story; sure, life will be more difficult on release but if handled correctly plenty of people leave prison never to return.

Ultimately by buying this book you have decided to at least start that journey correctly.

What we will try to do is open your eyes to the pitfalls of prison, introduce you to the procedures that are in place, show you what to avoid and how you will be tested by the system.

Your fear of the unknown will be far worse than the realities of prison.

We have seen young men, middle-aged men and senior members of society all pass through the gates with the same fear, trepidation and anxiety. As human beings, we are resilient and adapt very quickly to our surroundings, so what you are feeling at this stage is nothing new.

Many men have gone through this process, whether it's your first, second or third sentence the same fear, trepidation and anxiety is always prevalent, so you are in good company, we've all been there.

Chapter 1 - Court

Before going to court it is important that you ask your solicitor if your offence can carry a custodial sentence, if it does, you need to prepare yourself for the fact you may be remanded or sent to prison.

You might be told it is highly unlikely you will get a prison sentence but so much depends on the judge and how he perceives the offence - so our advice is that if prison is possible then pack a bag just in case.

Being prepared for prison at court is something that needs to be taken into consideration and goes beyond just taking a bag of clothes with you as we will outline now.

Getting your personal effects in order

If you rent your current property then you will need to consider letting your landlord or housing manager know and leave your keys with someone trusted.

If you are a council tenant then you may qualify for them to cover your rent for 12 months, but we advise you to speak to them before going to court.

If you chose not to sort this out before going to prison, you will be able to complete the procedure from prison, but, as with everything inside prison this will take much longer and will be the cause of additional stress, remember there is no internet access in prison, you don't have 24/7 access to a phone and mail takes longer to process.

It is important that you take a list of phone numbers, contact details and addresses of friends, family and acquaintances.

You will also have to consider that in prison you will have no direct access to your bank or normal business concerns so before going to court you will either have to give someone you trust power of attorney or make alternative arrangements.

Anything that you hold dear to you, must be secured in some way because as much as you may trust someone they may not realise how important certain things are and ultimately you could end up losing them.

We recommend that you pay particular attention to things of sentimental value like photographs, letters and trinkets.

This also applies to cats, dogs and cars.

Suggested kit bag

Here is a list of things we recommend having in your prison bag, you won't have this from day 1 in prison as it has to be checked in and then sorted by prison staff/officers to make sure there is nothing deemed as contraband (not allowed).

Also bear in mind how you want to present yourself in prison, having branded expensive clothes, watches or jewellery can make you a target. Our recommendation is to have unbranded items that are new but ultimately nothing that carries any value either sentimental or otherwise.

H.M.P - Help me prepare - A guide to prison for 1st timers and their families

We recommend that you put your name on everything you own in permanent marker, you will be surprised by how many people have the same jeans, tops and trainers.

No clothing that makes you look like a prison officer or any other staff will be permitted, no hoods, no caps, nothing that can cause injuries like steel toe cap boots or workwear, black jackets are forbidden.

The following list is a recommendation of what items are generally permitted into prisons - ultimately the prison will have the final say on the matter and will differ from prison to prison:

- Plain T-Shirts (no more than 7)
- Underwear 5 to 7 pairs (prison underwear is grim but is provided)
- Socks
- Trainers, no more than 3 pairs of footwear will be allowed (again these should be comfortable but expensive branded footwear will be targeted by thieves)
- Jumpers (no hoods, prison gets cold especially in winter, a jumper or two is advised if you will be there during winter months)
- Writing paper or pads - again you can be provided with this but it is a good way to pass time and letters become a good way of communication with friends and family on the outside.
- A pack of cards - they will help pass the time.
- A small amount of cash - this will be added to your prison spends and will be much quicker than having money sent in which means you will be able to spend within a week on canteen (see page 46)

- Any medication you need - a doctor's note accompanying it is beneficial but all medication will be checked through healthcare.
- Stamps - whilst the prison normally allows a letter a week free of charge you may decide to send more, you can purchase them via canteen.
- Toothbrush - again this will be provided but having a new toothbrush in the original packaging will be allowed.
- Your contacts list (names, numbers, addresses and date of births - your contacts will be approved by security for visits and calls and you will need to know all of this)

Most electrical items will not be permitted because the prison insists on them coming from approved manufacturers so it is advisable to purchase these through the prison catalogue system.

Toiletries are likely to be refused/held in storage. Ultimately it is up to the prison what they allow you to have, some will only allow you your own clothes when you become an enhanced prisoner.

Anything you do take - toothpaste, razors etc. are more likely to be allowed if they are in their original packaging and brand new. Nothing is a given though, the likelihood is the packaging will be opened during the checking in process and thoroughly checked anyway.

No product that contains alcohol will be permitted, mouthwash, aftershave etc. There will also be no aerosols permitted.

H.M.P - Help me prepare - A guide to prison for 1st timers and their families

Ultimately for the first couple of weeks, you will be expected to wear prison-issue clothing regardless of the regime, this is because every single item will be checked by prison security - it is worth noting that if you are found to be trying to smuggle anything in through your personal effects you may get additional charges and time added to your sentence.

Holding Cells

Once your fate has been decided and you have been found guilty you will be transferred to the holding cells, which lie beneath the court and will be similar to a police station cell.

This is when it hits home what has happened to you.

Some courts will send an insider to speak to you, an insider is normally from the prison you will be going to and will be a serving inmate. They will speak to you about the process and tell you what life is like there and what to expect.

This isn't always the case though so don't rely on it (this is a phrase that will become all too familiar as you read this book - everything is up to the prison and therefore subject to change).

Where an insider doesn't come to speak to you, it will be left to the court staff, these are normally hired by external companies and are not prison officers, some are brilliant, some are terrible. They do not work at the prison so probably don't know what the regime is like and will not be able to provide much help.

Generally, court staff will treat you as you treat them, so if you are polite and calm with them they will make your wait more bearable, some will even go out of their way to assist you as much as possible if you are rude and kick-off you can expect them to largely ignore you.

You may get a visit from your legal team, this will be brief as there is little they can do for you there and then.

You will probably get a sandwich and a drink but don't expect a 3-course meal or room service - what you will get is a taste of things to come... waiting, long waits and waiting some more.

Most courts will hold you until all cases are concluded, so you may not be moved for a few hours.

If you are lucky there will be a bus (prison van/sweatbox) leaving fairly soon after you are sent down but mentally you should prepare yourself to sit there for at least two to three hours.

You won't be permitted to have a fag at this time as courts in England and Wales are now 100% smoke-free sites no exceptions.

However long or short the wait, you will soon be on your way to prison.

Transport to prison

When asked about his first experience of sitting in a prison van in the courtyard outside the reception area of HMP Pentonville Terry said,

H.M.P - Help me prepare - A guide to prison for 1st timers and their families

"Honestly if they could have freed me at that one moment in time, I would never have committed another crime, my fear was palpable, my anxiety heightened by the baying shouts from the block windows which became increasingly more audible as the silence fell inside the van as the officers, with their steel toe cap boots, jingling keys and peak caps approached the van.

They call them sweatboxes for a reason, it could be minus 70°c outside and you would still sweat your bollocks off in one of those.

They are uncomfortable shoebox compartments that you get shoved into, a small porthole window that makes it impossible to see anything clear of the outside world, no fresh air, no idea where you're going, no idea how long it's going to take and no real concept of time.

No seatbelt either, just a hard wooden or plastic bench to sit on, so every time you go around a bend that you can't see approaching, so you slide around and get battered against the side, you can't get comfortable and you can't sit in one place, in fact, it's amazing how much you manage to move around in such a confined space.

They are designed to be a miserable, horrible and uncomfortable experience - if you are lucky you will be transported with a load of people who are in shock just like you and will complete the journey in contemplative silence but the chances are there will be at least one loud-mouth that will shout the odds, asking everyone what they are in for, how long they're doing and various other questions.

This is something you get used to as it is just a different way for them of coping with their situation.

Some people are quiet, some make jokes and some ask questions."

The period you wait at the court will be dictated by which prison you are due to go to and something which you have no control over, this can change at the drop of a hat depending on the circumstances.

For example, you could be ready to go to Winchester but an incident there means that your van will be re-routed, so instead you will be allocated a new prison within the catchment area, this is rare but it does happen so don't be alarmed if this happens to you.

A 10-minute journey just became 90 minutes, you probably won't be told either just stuffed in the box and driven.

The vans have several small compartments in them, rather like an old-fashioned train toilet in size except with a seat, not a toilet.

Seating around 10 people per van, each with their own "cell", you will have a security officer (G4S, Serco or similar) and a driver so thoughts of escape are futile.

From our own experiences of travelling in sweatboxes, we can tell you that it will be one of the few journeys' you will ever take where you pray for the van to crash.

Simply because there is a failsafe on each van, so when they tip-up or roll over the roof is released and this is your only viable method of escape through the escape hatch on the roof of the van located above each "cell" - we don't advocate any escape attempts but we guarantee these will be thoughts you have once inside the hell hole that is a sweatbox compartment.

H.M.P - Help me prepare - A guide to prison for 1st timers and their families

Don't expect to have a police escort unless you are a high-profile underworld figure, convicted terrorist or are classed as dangerous.

The van ride is slow, noisy and uncomfortable. There is no toilet so it pays to use the facilities in the court holding cell before you start the journey.

The van may not go straight to your prison and will stop at other prisons on the way. These stops all take time, but you can't make them go any faster by complaining.

Christopher Alston & Terry Ellis

Types of prison and prisoner

Categorisation

There are many types of prison within the UK, both private and publicly owned and these are best defined by the nature of the prisoners they keep.

Beyond the obvious split between male, female and juvenile, prisoners are split into categories according to the risk they represent to society and each other. There is also a split between Local Prisons and Dispersal Prisons.

A Local Prison is where you will be sent initially and where the assessment of you will take place. As its name suggests, a Local prison will be local to the area of the court where your trial is held.

The length of your sentence will determine which prison you are sent to. For sentences under 4 years, there is a good chance that you will remain in the "local" prison for most of your time inside but this isn't set in stone so there is every chance you will be moved on.

If your sentence is over 4 years then you will be moved to dispersal prison and potentially moved from there to another mainstream prison.

Ultimately the decision to move you falls to the holding prison, however, you can request a move but ultimately this decision will still be made by your current prison.

H.M.P - Help me prepare - A guide to prison for 1st timers and their families

It is as broad as it is long which type of prison is best, there is little to choose between them in terms of the regime they operate or the work/education opportunity they offer.

All prisoners are given a category that sets out how the prison system will handle them. At the most serious end for male prisoners are Category A prisoners and at the lower end are those deemed low risk and these are category D status.

To give you an idea of offences that would carry a category A status we have provided a list below:

- Murder
- Attempted murder
- Manslaughter
- Wounding with intent
- Rape
- Indecent assault
- Robbery and conspiracy to rob
- Firearms
- Importing Class A drugs
- Terror offences

Category A prisoners are further segregated into standard risk, high risk, and exceptional risk, based on their likelihood of escape or the risk they pose to other prisoners and staff.

Unless you are a Category A prisoner, most local prisons are B cat prisons and this will be your default categorisation until you are assessed and a sentence plan has been completed.

During your assessment and sentence planning, you may be deemed lower or higher risk and your categorisation adjusted.

At the other end of the scale from category A prisons are category D prison, these are referred to as open prisons.

Category D prisoners are defined as "those who can be reasonably trusted not to try to escape, and are given the privilege of an open prison."

It may take some time to progress through the various categories; if it is your first offence and it was a non-violent offence, drug-related crime, or fraud, you may be classified as a Cat D within months of being sent to prison.

The speed of progression depends on how you have reacted to the prison rules and regulations and how you have behaved whilst in custody.

However, while you are in prison your category will be regularly reviewed and towards the end of your sentence, you may well be re-categorised at a lower risk level and moved to an open prison to test your suitability for release.

Whilst open prison sounds like you are free, there are still rules and a regime to follow - you will have to attend role calls at regular intervals throughout the day and misbehaviour will soon see you sent back to closed conditions.

Once you have "failed" in open conditions you will find it can be held against you in the future, when courts look at bail conditions (if you find yourself back in front of a judge) they will consider this as being an example of someone who doesn't adhere to the rules.

It will also be difficult for you to convince a prison OMU (Offender Management Unit - page 46) to send you back to open conditions.

H.M.P - Help me prepare - A guide to prison for 1st timers and their families

And now you're a prisoner

The sweatbox has finally pulled into your destination; however, the wait isn't over yet this is only the beginning.

Everyone's bags will be taken off the van first for the initial scan, check and the relevant paperwork collected and completed.

The van will be held in the prison courtyard whilst these security checks are made.

After the van drivers have completed some basic paperwork you will be taken one by one into the reception area.

A prison officer will then put you into another holding cell, until you are called to the reception desk, take this opportunity to use the toilet as this could take anything up to two hours.

Reception/Check-In

The holding cell can "house" up to 20 men at a time and this will be your first introduction to being sized up.

This is where you will get your first experience of other prisoners trying to get information out of you and to look for any signs of weakness.

Don't give out too much personal information or too much about your history.

Remember you don't need to be rude because that in itself can cause you problems but you do need to be guarded.

Don't ever say how much money you have, don't reveal any drug or alcohol dependency, don't lend or borrow anything especially anything to do with smoking, don't reveal what medication you may be taking - these are things that could be used against you in the future.

One by one you will be called out of the holding cell to go through the process of check-in.

You will be asked to itemise your belongings, be thorough here because this is the only record you will have of what you brought in and should anything be lost, this is what you will need to make a claim.

This will form your property list (prop card) which you will have throughout your sentence, if you have items in your cell during a cell search that are not listed on this card they will be removed and you will be placed on an IEP or adjudication.

Once your belongings are checked in you will be subject to the first search.

Privacy that you may have once held dear will be violated in the prison system. The search is the first time this will happen because regardless of the crime, regardless of how pleasant you may have been with the staff and regardless of your personal preference you are about to be naked in front of 2 possibly 3 prison officers.

H.M.P - Help me prepare - A guide to prison for 1st timers and their families

The officers will be reassuring and will try to make it as unawkward as possible, they don't particularly enjoy it either but it is a necessary part of their job. They will have seen it all before so just listen and get on with it.

Every single prisoner is searched on entry to the prison, this is a full-body search; you will be asked to remove your clothes in a private area, watched by officers, they will then ask you to crouch and spread your cheeks to make sure there are no signs of cavity parcels.

You will also have to sit on a chair (the BOSS chair) that scans for phones, hopefully, you don't hear it beep - if they suspect you have some contraband inside you they may crack out the rubber gloves.

As well as a more intimate search you will also get put into an observation cell where you are monitored until you have passed any parcel.

After you have been searched, you will be moved onto the medical examination. This is just a sit down with a nurse who will ask you a series of questions about medical conditions and medication.

The nurse will also do an initial mental health assessment, this isn't in-depth but used as guidance to assess your mental wellbeing and your capacity to share a cell with another inmate.

At some point in this part of the journey, you will have your photo taken, be issued with your prison ID and your initial prison kit.

The kit will be prison-issue clothing, possibly some plastic cutlery, plates and either a smoker's pack (which may have been discontinued since the policy is now a smoke-free prison estate, if they still exist it will be a vape) or a non-smokers pack which is often tea bags, biscuits, perhaps some squash - don't expect much, you are not at a hotel.

The welcome pack is not free, this will be deducted from your private spends.

You will need to carry your prison ID with you at all times - it will have your picture, name and prison number.

You will need your prison number for people to contact you - shortly you will be offered your initial phone call, it is important that you provide people with your prison number for them to be able to contact you.

If you are reading this book then the person you are about to ring will be prepared and will need to write this number down.

The first phone call

Before moving to your first night wing, at some point in the induction process you will be allowed to make a phone call, for this to happen you will be given your PIN, you must memorise this and not let anyone have access to it or let anyone borrow it.

This is an important rule, you register all of your numbers on this pin and all of your phone credit. Certain prisoners may be banned from calling certain numbers i.e. victims or people involved in their criminal enterprise. They may attempt to circumnavigate this by putting numbers onto your pin.

H.M.P - Help me prepare - A guide to prison for 1st timers and their families

If you allow this to happen you may be placed on IEP or adjudication and in extreme circumstances you may face criminal charges and your future phone privileges will only be allowed under supervision.

This first phone call will have a 2-minute maximum duration, no longer and you will only get one call - this means if you get an answering machine that will count as your call.

The information you should give is your prison number, this is what people need when writing to you, sending money or when enquiring with the prison if they believe you are in danger.

This will be a hard call to make because this will be your first contact since learning you have been sent to prison.

Try to consider what you want to say before making the call, the 2 minutes will go by quickly.

Moving to your first wing

Once check-in has been completed and your phone call has been made you will be transferred to the first night wing.

This will be your first look at the prison; depending on where the wing is located you may get to walk down the walkways that interlink each section of the prison.

You will normally do this move when it is dark and the rest of the prison is shut down.

It will be completely normal for you to be anxious on this walk, the fear of the unknown in those first days and weeks is something everyone will be familiar with.

The first night

The first night in jail is probably the most difficult - if you are lucky the first night will be alone but prepare yourself to be sharing with someone, you won't have any say on who this is, as everyone is selected at random.

Even though the selection process is random they will take into consideration whether or not you are a smoker, similar in age, similar religious beliefs but this is very much a lottery.

To add to the lottery of potential cellmates you are about to realise that you have lost all of the privacy that you probably didn't realise was so precious to you… until now.

This lock-up period is where you will realise that going to the toilet alone is a thing of the past - cells have toilets in them, probably no shower and you will have a sink. A single TV between however many are in the cell (normally 2 people) and a kettle.

Some cells have the toilet separated by walls and a door - this is rare, most prisons have an open toilet and a shower curtain or small 4ft partition. Basically, privacy is a distant memory from here on.

H.M.P - Help me prepare - A guide to prison for 1st timers and their families

Another violation of privacy are the many spy holes that officers can use to see into the cell - there is the obvious one on the cell door but there will normally be one around the toilet so you can be viewed/observed at any given time.

You will be locked up for the evening at any time between 6 pm and 8 pm until the morning, lock-up time will differ from prison to prison and you are likely to not see an officer until the next morning.

You do have a call button in your cell, this notifies staff you are requesting to speak to someone, this is likely to be answered on your first night as people are more vulnerable but moving forward you can expect this to be ignored for long periods.

Persistent ringing of the cell bell is considered a punishable offence and can land you with an IEP.

Normal wing staff will be unable to open your door alone, having come to check your cell they would have to call a senior officer to open the door, in the event of sickness or an injury they would still need another senior officer (s.o) to attend.

If you are feeling depressed, suicidal and you need someone to speak to there are people called listeners who have been trained by the Samaritans and will come to talk to you.

We cover this later on in the book but briefly, this is a trained prisoner who will come and listen to your concerns, they are prisoners just like you so don't expect them to be able to change anything or get you anything - what you discuss is confidential but they will have to inform someone if you indicate that you may harm yourself, another prisoner or staff but most importantly if you indicate there is a risk of harm to a child or your family.

If you do arrive on the wing before the evening meals have been served (usually around 5 pm but this will differ from prison to prison) you are unlocked and asked to join the servery queue - the choice will be limited and most probably a vegetarian option, as you haven't yet completed a menu choice.

Depending on the prison you may also receive a breakfast pack - again don't get excited this will be a hot drink pack, some cereal or porridge oats and a small carton of milk (200ml, this has to last for your tea or coffee and your cereal so you will learn to be economical with it).

Meals are taken back to your cell to be eaten, you will have seen large dinner halls in films but this is based on American prisons, most local prisons don't have this, they are rare unless you are in an open prison.

Certain wings will have benches outside the cells but this is also rare.

The night itself is likely to pass incredibly slowly, this is true for even seasoned offenders so don't be surprised to be feeling scared, upset or any of the full spectrum of emotions you will feel - everyone is going through the same thing, some people will mask this better than others but rest assured every single person feels the same way.

The other thing that will hit you is the noise - we can't prepare you for this because every night is different but gone are the days of a quiet night's sleep.

H.M.P - Help me prepare - A guide to prison for 1st timers and their families

You are hyper-sensitive on that first night so you will hear every scream, every fight, every threat thrown across landings, every cry (yes people cry in prison, especially at night) and every single footstep from the patrolling guards - it is an assault on your senses - this gets easier as you move through prison but some nights will get to you more than others.

You will also become accustomed to the alarms - these are bells ringing constantly and will pierce through even the most laid back of prisoners as it can be likened to having seemingly never-ending tinnitus.

I won't list the reasons for these going off because that would be a book in itself but you will get used to these being a significant part of your life.

What you will realise too, is that mental health problems come alive at night inside prison and if you are fortunate enough not to be affected by these directly you will hear them.

The full range of mental health conditions can be found in prisons - be prepared to hear them every single night.

Once you have got through the night you will be unlocked in the morning - as with everything this varies from prison to prison, on the induction wing you can expect to be let out around 8 am - you are about to be confronted by the next privacy violation.

Showers, you will be offered the opportunity to get a shower. Think leisure centres of the 1980's and 1990's - communal rows of showerheads, the water might be hot but don't leave it too long because the luxury of hot water won't last long.

Our advice would be to wear flip flops if possible because another thing you will discover is that things like verruca's and athlete's foot are rife in this environment.

Preferably buy soap on a rope that you can tie around your neck so you don't accidentally drop it on the floor.

In the 15 years, I have been in prison I have never heard of one story of someone being raped in the showers, however, I have heard of 2 incidents of inmates being raped by their cellmates, but this is extremely rare, so forget the horror stories and whatever else you have seen in those prison films, Shawshank redemption it is not.

Induction

The induction process is mind-numbingly boring for the most part however, it gets you out of your cell and will help acclimatise you to life in prison.

Bear in mind that the process has to cater for all education levels and all levels of English so be prepared to go over things and be reassured that you can ask questions until you fully understand.

An orderly (which is what prisoner job titles are normally referred to as) will probably take the induction, they are prisoners just like you and they are well placed to introduce you to life inside the prison.

H.M.P - Help me prepare - A guide to prison for 1st timers and their families

Depending on how trusted the orderly is, they can also have some say on which wing to send you to. Those new to prison or who are considered vulnerable either due to their mental health or simply the fact they are first-time prisoners may be located on the VP (vulnerable person) wing, these are commonplace in most prisons now.

The induction process is an important part of introducing you to prison life, it's your way to get all the necessary timetables that highlight when you can and can't do certain activities, you will be introduced to the prison rules and procedures and you will be offered a gym induction.

Even if you think you will never need or want to use the gym, we recommend you take the induction anyway.

The gym is a good way to keep your mental health in check and will help you fight depression, we highly recommend it especially if you have never been before, by doing the induction at the earliest possible opportunity it will mean that you can access it when you are ready.

On a final note about induction if you happen to be the only first timer in the induction group then a lot of the info will be rushed through and glossed over because officers and orderlies will sense people aren't paying attention.

If you are unsure about anything, ask now, the process of getting information in prison takes time - you will get used to hearing "not my job today", "don't know ask x, y or z", "you need to fill out an app for that".

Take this opportunity to make sure you understand.

As part of your induction, you will meet with the chaplaincy, the drug team, the medical team, education, probation, gym and perhaps someone from the IMB (Independent Monitoring Board page 109).

First timer and at-risk wing

Most prisons will have one of these, they are designed specifically for prisoners that are considered to be most vulnerable.

These wings are sometimes referred to as the VP wing or the drug-free wing, this isn't to be confused with the Vulnerable Prisoner wing that we discuss later on.

To be allocated on this wing it is likely that you will have to sign a compact (like a contract) agreeing to several conditions and the wing will operate a zero-tolerance policy to break that compact.

Some of the general conditions that you will agree to are no violence, no drugs, no bullying, there will be some general hygiene standards to maintain and you will be expected to help keep the landings and association areas free of rubbish and abuse.

If you are worried about prison and you want to keep your head down and just get on with your sentence, we recommend requesting to be placed on the VP wing during your induction.

There is no shame in wanting to avoid the trouble and violence that plague prisons but if you want to keep yourself out of that you need to make sure that you don't instigate it.

H.M.P - Help me prepare - A guide to prison for 1st timers and their families

Hygiene and the complete lack of privacy

Your complete lack of privacy is something we have already mentioned but we really can't stress how little you have in prison, but like most things, you will learn to live with it.

You will likely have a sink and a toilet in your cell, as described earlier you will need to learn to go to the toilet in front of your cellmate, you will also have to live with the sounds and smells of chocolate flavoured flatulence and shit fingered graffiti on the walls due to the poor quality of the budget toilet roll provided.

Because you are sharing the toilet, it's important to do your part in keeping it clean, you will need to ask for cleaning materials from the wing office, but letting it build-up is a recipe for an uncomfortable life. No one wants to sleep next to a pile of shit.

Most people will be happy to agree to a cleaning rota of the toilet.

Showers are another thing done communally, some prisons have divides between the showers but not many, some wings even have a bath or two but this is the main shower block so don't expect any privacy there either.

Your hygiene is important, poor hygiene invites problems, no one wants to be told that they smell, if your cellmate or another prisoner has been putting up with smelling your sweat daily then eventually they will snap and you will end up in a confrontation.

We recommend that for the sake of a roll-on deodorant and a bar of soap (which the prison provides) this scenario is easily avoided.

Having good hygiene will also help your mental wellbeing, the guards will be more likely to interact with you and if you do have an issue with someone else's stench then bringing it up is easier if you are generally clean and tidy.

Another issue with prison is that you will be surrounded by dirty bastards, especially when you get to your first cell, new cell, next cell, last cell, whichever cell you are going to, you should prepare yourself to have to clean it.

You can get annoyed, angry, upset, disgusted and so on but ultimately it will make no difference; whatever mess you walk into, it will be your responsibility to clean it.

No one will do anything for you in prison.

Vulnerable Prisoner Wing

Most people will arrive at this section and think, it doesn't apply to me and skip past it.

Whilst you may wish to do that our goal has always been to educate with this book, the following is written by a former prison officer and whilst the information is aimed at a particular type of offender there is plenty any inmate can take away from it.

We wanted this book to be as inclusive as possible and the reality is that people go to prison for sexually motivated crimes and crimes against children.

H.M.P - Help me prepare - A guide to prison for 1st timers and their families

If you fall into this category then your fear is just as relevant as anyone's, therefore we asked Joe Chapman to write the following section of the book. Joe has 44 years of experience in the prison service, he worked for a large portion of that with Vulnerable Prisoners and has a support group for those prisoners.

"It is said that no one truly knows a nation until one has been inside its jails. A nation should not be judged by how it treats its highest citizens, but its lowest ones."
— Nelson Mandela

And, in the prison hierarchy, there is no person lower than a sex offender!

For many, there is no worse feeling than receiving the guilty verdict in court, and for those convicted of sexual offences, there is no journey more feared, as they enter the parallel universe known as the Prison and Probation System.

As Star Treks Mr Spock would say, "There's life Jim, but not as we know it".

You may be sent down immediately, or you may face that uncertain period of waiting before being sentenced, but either way, the day will arrive when you are taken down to the "Holding Cells" ready to await your transfer to prison.

You may receive a visit from your brief (barrister) but otherwise, you will be left alone with your thoughts. Whatever you may have heard about prison life, and particularly how Sex Offenders may be treated, having been convicted of a sexual offence you automatically became a VP (Vulnerable Prisoner), and the Prison Service and all agencies who are contracted to work for them, should be aware of the legislation that is in place to cover your protection.

I say should be, because you must never take it for granted that the person who has a duty of care towards you will always be well informed.

It is in your interests to arm yourself with as much knowledge as you can, so that you know what should, or should not, be happening daily.

BE ON YOUR GUARD:

Once you leave the dock, and you are being escorted to the cells, that duty of care begins right there.

Be prepared for abuse from other prisoners as they pass by, or if they are held in adjacent cells. As a convicted sex offender you immediately become vulnerable to extreme verbal abuse, and physical abuse. Although you should be protected by your status and not be placed at risk, you need to be on your guard for any weak link in the security that might allow other prisoners to get to you.

Usually, you are held on your own in a cell, which lets others know you are under protection and they form their own conclusions. If you find yourself sharing a cell, it is guaranteed that the other person will also be a VP, although he may not be convicted of sexual offences. VP prisoners can also be prisoners who are being bullied or informants under protection.

The officers at the court work for private companies, so they will have limited knowledge of the prison you are going to. For security reasons, they may decide not to tell you where you are going, but some will. However, communication with them will be minimal.

BE PATIENT:

H.M.P - Help me prepare - A guide to prison for 1st timers and their families

You will be well advised to expect very little in the first few hours of your sentence; therefore, you are not going to be disappointed.

Be prepared for a lot of waiting and thinking. If you are locked in with another prisoner, just stick to a pleasant chat and avoid giving any information about your case, from here on it has to be limited to those you know you can trust, and they are in short supply.

If you are kept waiting over the lunch period, you will get a basic meal. It's worth eating it, no matter how unpalatable it might look as it could be your only meal for hours. Make sure you use the toilet before getting into the prison van (sweatbox), as there isn't one on board.

Once the prison van arrives you will be processed and loaded into a small compartment, no bigger than a standard toilet with a single uncomfortable seat. The ride will be long, slow, and pretty painful, with lots of shouting from other prisoners, don't be tempted to join in, it is much better and safer to sit and listen. If your case was high profile you could be the topic of conversation, and other prisoners will probably have guessed you are onboard.

According to the length of the journey, you will probably have been quiet for several hours, and if the van stops at several prisons you will sit and wait as they unload.

ROLE STRIPPING:

The first person you will meet when you arrive will be the "Reception screw" and he, or she, will explain everything you have to do as you are checked into jail. By now you will have experienced being cuffed up (often uncomfortably) and getting several rub-down searches. But in jail, you will go through a thorough "strip search" where you will remove all of your clothing, and be asked to sit in a special seat, called a Boss Chair, which checks you have no items hidden inside your body.

During a strip search, there should be two members of staff (of the same gender) present, and you should not be left completely naked. Normally they search from the waist up and then give you an upper-body garment before removing everything from the waist down.

The reception process was once referred to as "Role Stripping" whereby your identity outside is replaced with the identity of a convicted prisoner. You will be given a prison number, which will be yours for the rest of your life, and just like your NHS number, it will be used to identify you as you progress through the system.

At this stage, it is worth noting that most Prison Officers will conduct themselves in a professional, and reasonably respectful manner, they have a job to do and although appearing abrupt they will respond positively to you if you refer to them respectfully as "Sir", "Boss" or "Gov", at this stage "Mate" "Pal" "Bruv" etc is best avoided.

Within an hour or so of arriving you should have a medical examination, and you will have plenty of forms to fill in, recording the personal property you have, and agreeing to "Prison Compacts" which explain the rules you are required to abide by. You will be photographed and given your Prison ID card, which you must produce at all times when asked (normally work around your neck on a lanyard).

There will be lots of questions to answer during this period to find out if you are a danger to yourself or others, and the assessment of you begins from this point onwards, throughout your sentence. It is important for Prison Staff to identify your state of mind before they

H.M.P - Help me prepare - A guide to prison for 1st timers and their families

locate you, and to know what your anxieties are. If there are any major concerns health-wise, or you have any serious health issues, make sure you let Prison Officers and Health Professionals know.

WHO DO YOU THINK YOU ARE TALKING TO?

Be aware of who the people are that you are talking to, at any given time, as much as possible. As you begin your sentence it will be really useful to begin a daily diary of your journey. But bear in mind that the diary will be read by prison staff, and could easily be stolen and read by others, so you should keep your entries to basic information, and avoid writing about other prisoners or criticising staff in them.

Prison Officers do enjoy reading notes that praise their performance but notes that cast doubts on their parenthood are not well received.

In most jails you will be introduced to a prisoner who is a mentor, sometimes referred to as a listener and this prisoner will supply you with more accurate information about the prison and where you will be living.

You may be given a short phone call, which only lasts a couple of minutes, just to let somebody in your support network (partner, family, or friend) know you have arrived safely.

But, sex offenders are subject to strict public protection assessments, so you may not get a call until your numbers have been checked out by the prison Security Department and Public Protection Office, which can take anything from 24 hours to several days. Each of the people you intend to call will be given a personal Pin Number, which will be added to your Pin Card, for use on the prison telephone.

Guard this Pin Card with your life, and don't let it fall into the hands of any other prisoner.

BECOMING AN INMATE:

The title "Inmate" is not that accurate as you may be "In", but you will not all be "mates"

You will quickly discover, rather through trial and error who you feel you can get on with and who you can't, and finding somebody you can trust is like finding a needle in a haystack at first, but they are there.

When you finally reach your wing, often referred to as a "VP Unit", you will be passed over to Wing Officers who will show you to your cell. If you are lucky, you will have a single cell, but otherwise, you will be sharing with another prisoner, and you get no choice as to who that person might be. You are initially given the bare minimum when you arrive (blankets, pillow, a plastic plate, plastic mug, plastic cutlery and some prison-issue clothing, not made to measure!

It is likely, but not certain, that you will be taken to an "induction spur" where all new prisoners spend the first week or two of their sentences. The officer will then lock you in the cell, and leave you to your own devices, while they record your details in the wing office, and make entries on the C-Nomis system (this is a data collection programme that records everything about you from the moment you arrive.

Getting to know your cellmate will be your first major challenge, and he/she may be just as new to it as you or may have been in the system for years. You make agreements with them about sleeping arrangements, storage space and cell cleaning etc.

Cells vary so much in different prisons, so what you will receive can't be determined easily, some have poor ventilation and sanitary arrangements, whilst others can have toilets and in cell showers, even in cell telephones. It all depends on the prison you are sent to.

There is some thought given to prisoners who have to share, and the prison officers will try to pair you up with somebody reasonable, to avoid future problems, but there can be occasional problems.

DAILY ROUTINES:

Prisons all work on strict timetables and timetables vary greatly, also the amount of time you spend locked behind your door will depend on local staffing levels and resources.

As stated earlier "expect very little, and the rest will be a bonus."

The first night inside often passes very slowly, and you are bound to worry about the conditions you face, but generally speaking, VP Units are free from violence, Prison Officers will be concerned about your safety, and are trained to monitor your situation closely. It would be wrong to say you won't experience trouble, but if you go looking for it you will certainly find it.

You should be allocated a Personal Officer at some point, and hopefully, you will be able to spend time getting to know them, as they will be your first port of call when you want questions answered, but that doesn't mean other officers can't answer them in their absence. Communication with the screws varies greatly, from those who will chat in a friendly manner to you as often as they can, to those who will barely notice you.

You will soon get to know who is worth talking to and who is not.

The nature of the induction process varies greatly also, but they will cover the same topics. You will attend talks and presentations about the prison rules and guidelines, what jobs or education opportunities exist, and details about visiting rules. You will also learn about getting clothes brought in, how to book visits, how to get money sent in, canteen timetables, gym timetables, library etc. You will also meet the chaplaincy, the drug team, the medical team, education, probation, and gym.

You will soon find that the Offender Management Unit (OMU), psychologists and Probation are a major part of a Sex Offenders staff team, and you will certainly meet one or more of them in the first couple of months.

If you are serving more than 12 months, they will be busy preparing your Sentence Plan and an assessment of your risk called an OASYS, which will follow you through your sentence, and predicts your future risk to the public and others.

At this stage you will quickly learn that living on a VP unit is not the nightmare you imagined it to be …. Of course, there are going to be lots of seemingly petty rules, and restrictions on your liberty and rights, but this is what you signed up to when you committed the offences, and living on "the main" wings would not be something that most sex offenders would welcome.

We understand that there are those who are maintaining their innocence. However, the fact remains that you have been convicted and must be treated as guilty unless there is a successful appeal.

H.M.P - Help me prepare - A guide to prison for 1st timers and their families

Apps (not phone apps)

Prisons have evolved over the years but the same can't be said for the officers, the biggest bug bearer for the prisoners is still being told by the staff to fill out an app (application form) every time you ask them a question.

If an officer doesn't want to answer a simple question or carry out a basic request they will ask you to fill out an app.

An app is a formal request form that is used inside the prison.

A general app will cover 90% of the requests you will want to make, there will be specific apps for medical, complaints and specific departments.

Sometimes you will find yourself filling out an app for an app, they are annoying and we firmly believe they are there to test you.

However, you will quickly realise that they are a necessary evil in the current prison setup because nothing gets done without an app.

They are pre-printed forms that consist of 3 pieces of carbon copy paper, it is important that you keep these copies for your records, they are normally collected from the wing office and returned to an officer there every morning.

Don't expect an immediate answer either, your requests are not dealt with quickly in prison, this can be testing for a lot of people. You will also learn that a lot of stuff is paper-based and with that much paper floating around, some of it gets lost depending on the officer dealing with it.

So, writing duplicate apps and chasing lost apps with your carbon copies will become a skill you learn quickly.

If your app hasn't been lost you will get an answer within 5 days or so, depending on the prison your answer will arrive on the same form you sent and it will either be collected from the office or slipped under your door.

If the answer is not what you wanted there is a process of appeal and a procedure for complaint (another form) which we will cover later on.

On the next page we have made up an example of the prison-issue general application form, this has been designed only as a reference.

H.M.P
Help Me Prepare

An inmates guide to prison

Prisoner General Application Form

Prison number: [　　　] Name: [　　　] Cell Location: [　　　]

Date of application: [　　　] Application taken by: [　　　]

What do you need us to deal with:

Staff to write: Which department or who the application is going to: [　　　]
Date arrived at department: [　　　]

Reply (required within 5 working days:

Signature:　　　Name:　　　Date:

Date received and logged in the book by unit coordinator [　　　]

Pitfalls - What to avoid in your first few days

The first few days can define your sentence, we don't write this to scare you but to educate you, to give you the information from former inmates, their families and officers.

The first days involve a lot of sizing up, you size up others and they size you up.

Everyone is out for themselves and in these first few days, you are likely to find your first fake friend. No different to life on the outside, people latch onto people they think can benefit themselves.

Avoid giving out too much personal information, don't share anything, especially if you need it or want to see it again.

If you want to give someone a biscuit that is up to you but don't expect it back, if someone is familiar with the prison system and they lend or give you anything they will expect it back with interest.

Get used to the concept of "double bubble": borrow a cigarette, expect to return two, take 1 pack of smokes and return 2.

You will also be starting to realise that everything is currency - there is a market for everything. An example could be you want a can of pop - this might be on offer on a wing for 10 cereal packs or 1 sleeping tablet.

For this reason, you mustn't waste any tradeable resource in your first few days.

We must point out that it is illegal to trade in this way but it is commonplace in prison. If you lend or borrow anything that is on your property card or have anything that is not on your property card then you and the other person will be placed on an IEP or adjudication.

Avoid confrontation, the guards are also sizing you up and if you are perceived to be a trouble maker you might end up on a rougher wing than you had hoped.

There may be something you need, if you are coming off a certain drug or alcohol and are dependent on it so you may seek these out, you may need tobacco or vape fluid, could be anything and there will be someone who can get it for you.

The problem is, this is how people saddle themselves in debt, your spending money will take anything from a week to a month to sort out - you will be limited to what you can spend too.

If you owe someone an amount of money on your canteen sheet (this is how items are bought and sold) that will increase each week that you don't pay.

For example; you bought a heroin replacement that cost £10, people will exchange things too but normally you will owe £10 of canteen to whoever you bought the heroin from.

If your money hasn't come in, they don't want to wait, so you have now become in debt, the punishment for not paying might be doubling what you owe, it will also likely involve violence.

The other option is that you pay the debt by having to do something for them, this could be some form of errand where you have to hurt someone or take the risk of delivering drugs to someone or collecting another debt.

The most likely outcome will be that they will put pressure on one of your family members to deposit the money in an account or in some cases send someone to visit a family member and demand the money.

All this comes at a cost so a £10 debt can become £100 because they will now charge you for sending someone round.

Due to the ease of obtaining a mobile phone in prison, these scenarios are becoming more and more frequent and easy to arrange, so be warned.

You don't want to owe anyone anything in prison, even if you can afford whatever you want to buy, you open yourself up to problems when you get into these sorts of deals.

Your first proper wing - the first few weeks

After you have completed your stay on the induction wing, the duration of this will vary between one night and one week depending on the influx of new arrivals and what regime the prison has adopted, you will be moved over to your first proper wing.

If you enjoyed the first night(s) in a single cell that will all change today, as you're now entering the main wing where double bang-up is standard practice.

The only exception to this is if you are a high-risk prisoner or you have a complex medical need.

Getting a cellmate is stressful for both of you, this doesn't change for the duration of your time in prison because you will always be wondering what the next person will be like.

That isn't to say you can't get a good cellmate and you won't have a laugh but if everyone is honest then you want your own space and it doesn't matter if you are padded up with the best guy in the world, you are both going to get on each other's tits at some point.

Compromise is essential if you are to survive prison.

The UK Government recently said most men in prison would prefer to share a cell - they wouldn't! This is just another lie they tell families of prisoners to make it look like they are doing the right thing.

The Government likes to pretend there are not the problems in prison that currently exist, the rhetoric is that things aren't that bad, so we will break it to you now, most Victorian prisons in London and across the UK estate (Scrubs, Pentonville, Wandsworth, Brixton etc.) are a cockroach, silverfish and rodent-infested but an accepted part of the living conditions you will have to put up with.

From my experience in HMP Pentonville, my sink and personal space were constantly invaded by cockroaches, one fell on my face during the night and woke me up, I had to bag up all of my clothes in plastic bags and tie the bags to prevent them getting into my clothes constantly.

This was a never-ending battle between me and my six-legged nemesis.

The establishment will only ever fumigate one cell at a time which allows the infestation to continue because they never wipe them out as they would need to shut down an entire wing to get on top of the problem.

Because space is at a premium this is something that will never be allowed to happen, the space doesn't exist to relocate an entire wing. Added to that is the fact the prison service doesn't have the manpower either to facilitate such a move even if the space was available.

The good news is, there are more modern prisons and if you arrive at one of these then the chances are your stay will be infestation free.

The questions you will have about sharing is the same as your cellmate:
- Does he snore?

- Does he smoke?
- Is he going to rob my stuff?
- Will he want to watch what I like?
- Does he smell?
- Will we get on?
- Does he have mental health problems?
- Is he a drug user?
- Will he invite his friends in and out during association?

You're both thinking about it.

If you carry any prejudice about people you will do well to drop it before you go into prison because you encounter all types of people and whilst the prison will try and avoid putting a person of colour in with an admitted racist you will meet people on the wing from all backgrounds.

There is a hierarchy on the wings similar to life on the outside, if you avoid confrontation on the outside then the chances you will avoid it inside but you will need to learn to bite your tongue and you have to let the little things slide if you want to complete your sentence with as little grief as possible.

Your first cell and cellmate

Single cells are reserved either for people who are a risk to others, certain medical needs or as an earned privilege, it is possible to work your way up to a single cell.

So, unless you have a specific need you are about to get a roommate.

Cells will consist of either bunk beds or single beds; the Government will have the public believe that 2 man bang-up is as packed as a cell can get. 3 man bang-up is not unusual too and up to 4 man bang-up has been reported due to overcrowding.

2-man bang is the most common but when you hear of a prison increasing capacity they haven't suddenly built more cells they have just added beds to existing cells.

You will have to learn to compromise, there is 1 TV between however many are in the cell and because the TV becomes one of the biggest ways to pass time you will need to agree on what you are both watching.

Remember that you will be "banged up" for up to 23 hours a day so it isn't like you can get up and walk around if you are frustrated or need to escape a smell or annoying habit.

Bang-up

Bang-up is the affectionate term for being locked in your cell.

Since savage cuts to prison budgets happened the current crop of officers will ensure that you are banged up for as long as they can get away with it and they will use any excuse to have a longer bang-up.

It isn't completely the fault of the officers, experienced staff that knew how to run a wing were lost and the turnover of staff is such that you now have lots of officers with a small amount of experience on the job.

They have also cut staff numbers and the reality is that it is hard for officers to have proper unlock regimes with so few staff and have it safely managed.

If you are in a regime that allows more than just exercise and association time, then you can expect to be unlocked and given more time out of your cell.

However, if there is unrest either on your wing or another wing elsewhere in the prison that takes officers off your wing, you can expect to be banged up for longer periods.

So never get used to time out of your cell because bang-up is always just around the corner.

Learning to manage your bang-up time is a key to completing your sentence, use your time effectively - Terry the co-author of this book and author of the UK bestseller Living amongst the beast used his bang-up time to write 2 books.

Reading and educating yourself is a great way to pass time, the library has plenty of books to teach yourself new skills or languages.

Regime

The regime is the routine, it's what happens and when. In B cat prisons where most of you will be heading the current status quo is around 23 hours bang-up.

What this means is you get 30 mins association time, this is where you are on the wing out of your cell, table tennis and pool are probably the two things you will find most familiar.

Prisons tend to lump the evening meal into association time so you will have to factor in eating your dinner too in this time.

You will also get 30 mins to exercise outside or at least be offered it, this is a legal requirement to get 30 minutes of outdoor fresh air a day.

Despite it being a legal requirement under the human rights act you will be surprised how often you don't get it.

This has been a bone of contention for many inmates and has led to several flair ups over the years. It doesn't take much for exercise to be stopped, rain, snow and even high winds are all reasons they will stop outdoor time.

Now, not all prisons are the same and the regime will very much vary from prison to prison, sometimes it will be different from wing to wing - if you have ended up on a wing with a load of dickheads that can't be let out for more than 2 minutes without fighting, the chances are the staff will keep the wing on as basic a regime as they can get away with.

There are plenty of other opportunities to get out of your cell during the day, so don't read this and think you have to be locked up for 23 hours every single day.

We talk about getting out of your cell later on but to give you an idea there is:
1. Work
2. Education

3. Gym
4. Healthcare
5. Visits
6. Faith
7. Library
8. OMU

We cover all of these in detail later on in the book, just escaping the cell for an hour is a relief so knowing how to use the various facilities is a good way of breaking up the week, especially if you are in a basic regime with limited free time.

IEP - Incentives and Earned Privileges

Every prisoner has a status that is linked to behaviour - your IEP status. You will be given your first one at induction and it will be classed entry status.

There are 4 statuses Basic, Entry, Standard and Enhanced - different prisons may call them different things but essentially, they are the same.

The IEP status will determine how many visits you are allowed, access to a TV, how much money you can spend on your canteen, whether or not you can wear your own clothes etc.

As you progress through your sentence you move up the IEP status providing you follow the rules and generally behave acceptably.

If you don't follow the rules or you are generally a dick with staff and prisoners then you are more likely to be moved down.

They don't have to move you one status at a time when going down - so if you are enhanced you can drop to basic depending on what you have done.

During your time in prison the officers may issue warnings for minor things, these are not recorded on your prison record they are just like verbal warnings.

However, for persistent stuff or more serious offences, you may get a "nicking" also known as an adjudication. These will go on your prison record and will involve some kind of punishment.

For the more minor things, this punishment could be loss of canteen, moved to basic IEP status, reductions in visits and things like that.

If it is very serious you may find yourself in front of a judge.

Prisons have visiting Judges and if your offence is deemed serious enough it can be passed on to the judge and they can give you additional days on your sentence.

You could also commit an offence that could be considered a criminal offence, for example stabbing someone. This would involve a police investigation and subsequent trial.

The same could be applied to drugs and mobile phones in prison, so it is good to question whether getting involved in this is worth it.

You may have taken the decision not to get involved with phones, drugs or contraband in prison but your cellmate might. If he then hides his contraband in your belongings and the cell is spun (searched), you will likely end up with charges, so be vigilant, this does and has happened on many occasions.

Personal Officer

At some point in your first few weeks normally in the first few days, you will be allocated a personal officer.

The officer will normally work on your wing so if you move wings the chances are you will also get a new officer.

Your personal officer is your point of contact within the prison and like with most things in life, you get brilliant one's and shit one's (not so good ones).

If you're new, a good officer will come and seek you out, initiate contact and generally help you settle in, a bad one will wait for you to find them and then most probably fob you off with excuses and broken promises.

In the defence of some officers, they are also new to the job and they don't understand the value of having a reliable officer to help you through the sentence.

Officers also have to be mindful that not everyone is genuine and some prisoners are looking to manipulate them rather than seek genuine help and support.

Your personal officer will give you a reference for any jobs you apply for in the prison and will advise on whether your IEP should be increased or decreased.

Try and establish a good rapport with your PO because they can help you, whilst they are not there to be at your beck and call and their duties are limited they are the person in the prison that will influence your record.

Due to limited time and the number of prisoners they will oversee, PO's generally only note down the bad things and not the good things. So, your prison record will always look more negative than it perhaps should.

OMU (Offender Management Unit) - Sentence plan

The OMU is the department in the prison that influence your journey through the system the most.

However, despite having the most influence on your sentence they are the one department that will see you in person the least.

They base 90% of their decisions and work on your prison record and work/education record, which makes having a clean record imperative to succeed.

The OMU will be responsible for producing what is called a sentence plan, this is a plan you are expected to work towards to progress through prison and depending on your offence it may include behavioural programs, post-release monitoring, drug and alcohol rehabilitation/awareness and violence reduction courses - the list is endless and there will be little consideration given to whether or not your current prison offers these courses.

The sentence plan can look impressive and even inspire you to believe that the system is geared to help you, however, due to a lack of joined-up thinking and cooperation between prison, probation and community support when you leave prison the support simply isn't there which is why there is such a revolving door of recidivism.

Whilst in prison the sentence plan is an important tool in helping you progress and you will only be successful in prison if you embrace the plan and action the points within it.

Meals

Food in prison can be hit and miss, mostly miss. The daily budget is small per prisoner and the quality of food is reflected in this.

The budget is around £1.87 per prisoner per day for food, most food is bulk bought and cooked but don't expect restaurant-quality food.

You will order your meals in advance using a weekly meal form - this will contain several choices each day for your afternoon meal and evening meal.

If you fail to return your form on time, you don't fill it out or it gets lost then you are given the default option which is normally the vegetarian option because they have to cater for all diets.

This can't be changed once your choice is in and the servery where you collect your food won't change it on the day.

The food is prepared and served by prisoners with assistance from outside staff employed by the prison. The kitchen is monitored by prison officers and prisoners are often subject to searches on leaving the kitchen to ensure they are not smuggling anything out.

Breakfast is normally handed out at the evening meal and will be a cereal pack, milk and a hot drink pack.

If you are unfortunate enough to be inside at Christmas or during a religious festival then the prison will try and cater for this within the agreed budget.

Occasionally you may have an outside group come into the prison to serve food, Buddhists, Sikhs and Muslims are among the religious groups that come into certain prisons and provide meals on one-off occasions.

Even though you are provided with 3 meals a day, prepare to go hungry because the portion sizes reflect the budget prison are given.

Most men will supplement their weekly meals with canteen purchases. The biggest seller is dried noodles.

You will become an expert kettle chef in prison as you learn how to make noodle curry in a conventional kettle and warm baked beans on radiators.

Prisoners demonstrate an incredible amount of resourcefulness with regards to supplementing their meals, never has so much been made by so few, using only a kettle!

Some wings may have the luxury of a microwave, this is a blessing and becoming or getting to know an expert microwave chef will make your stay in prison far more palatable.

Kit day / allocation

Kit day or wash day is when your wing is allocated to exchange their prison-issue kit for clean stuff and to put your own washing into the laundry.

During your induction, you will be issued a certain amount of prison-issue stuff. Normally it will be as follows:

1. Prison boxers
2. Socks
3. 2 pairs of jogging bottoms
4. 2 prison T-shirts
5. 2 prison sweatshirts
6. 1 pillowcase
7. 1-bed sheet
8. 1 blanket
9. 1 Towel
10. 1 face towel

Kit change is done on a one for one basis, so to get a fresh bed sheet you have to bring a bedsheet.

For your clothing and personal kit, you can get a wash bag, write your name on it and then put the bag into the laundry.

The kit will be washed and returned to you on the next kit day.

The schedule for wash days will be available from the wing office and will vary from prison to prison.

It is always important to have a good rapport with the guys in the laundry and the odd mars bar or can of pop will go a long way to ensuring that they never lose your stuff.

Canteen - Spends

Canteen is the weekly shopping system where you can use your earned or private money to buy various items. Below is an example form to give you an idea of what they look like:

Price	Item	IC	Qty	Price	Item	IC	Qty	Price	Item	IC	Qty
£2.79	Corned Beef 340g(H)	189272		£1.99	Mango Pulp 850g	101773		£16.99	Amino Load 1kg	218704	
£1.29	Chicken Sausages 400g(H)	189206		£0.79	Economy Evaporated Milk(V)	145264			**STATIONERY**		
£1.65	Hot&Spicy Hot Dogs 400g(H)	201104		£1.99	Carnation Condensed Milk(V)	525972		£1.00	A4 Col Therapy 32 Designs	201482	
£1.45	Princes Mince Beef Tin 392g	634374		£0.76	Thick Cream Tin 170g(V)	616623		£1.99	8" Pencil Case inc Pencils	201487	
£1.59	Princes Hot Chicken Curry 400g	128106		£0.95	Coconut Milk 400ml(VE,GF)	204572		£0.35	Blue Biro Pen	041125	
£0.89	Beans & Sausages 395g	187854		£0.69	Economy Rice Pudding(V)	144917		£0.21	BIC Black Biro Pen	041146	
£1.19	Hamburgers in Gravy 425g	134406		£0.49	Golden Ac Creamy Yogurt(V)	144671		£0.04	Clear Multi Punched Pocket	185617	
£2.59	Stewed Steak 392g	127252		£0.40	Economy Custard Powder	146634		£0.15	Manilla Envelope C4	090294	
£1.79	Granovita Nut Luncheon(VE)	103657		£1.45	Ambrosia Custard Tetra (V)	097808		£0.40	DL Envelopes 10 Pack	140618	
£0.35	#3 Ko-lee Inst Ndle Curry(V,H)	148222		£0.95	Angel Del Butterscotch(V)	125422		£0.99	A4 Refill Pad 100 Sheets	202597	
£0.35	#3 Ko-lee Inst Ndle Beef(H)	148224		£0.89	Angel Delight Str/berry(V)	016987		£1.49	Sketch Pad A4	140604	
£0.43	#4 TasteSen Thai Chck Curry(H)	140612		£0.59	Strawberry Jelly Block	003004		£0.59	Writing Pad A5	140809	
£0.43	#4 TasteSen Chicken (H)	189228		£1.09	Str/berry Jelly Crystals(VE)	184425		£0.19	Rubber Tipped Pencil	092227	
£0.43	#4 TasteSens King Prawn(H)	194783		£0.59	Table Salt 750g	127009		£0.69	SE Glue Stick	191864	
£0.43	#4 TasteSons Mixed Veg(V,H)	194758		£0.79	Ground Black Pepper 25g	578286		£0.39	Plastic Ruler	191933	
£0.43	GoC Hot&Spicy Noodles(V,H)	143682		£0.79	Garlic Powder 100g	805374		£1.35	Coloured Pencils 18s	175762	
£0.59	Noodle Pot Snack Curry (H,V)	090777		£0.79	Crushed Chillies 100g	128188		£0.89	Coloured Felt Tip Pens 12s	190815	
£0.59	Noodle Pot Roast Chicken (H)	090775		£0.79	Chilli Powder 100g	664680		£1.49	Highlighter Pen 4Pk	195665	
£0.75	Smash Original (V)	677180		£0.69	Garam Masala 100g(VE)	665976		£0.19	Metal Pencil Sharpener	093788	
£1.00	ES Basmati Rice 500g	182407		£0.99	Hot Curry Powder 100g	189224		£0.19	Eraser	093792	
£1.45	Ko-lee Egg Noodles 375g	104872		£0.59	Tandoori Masala 100g	165252		£1.00	A4 Ringbinder	192072	
£0.75	HS Macaroni 500g	199896		£0.59	Paprika Powder 100g(VE)	805366			**RELIGIOUS ITEMS**		
£0.75	HS Spaghetti 500g	199902		£0.49	Ground Coriander 100g	805341		£2.99	Stanbul Perfumed Oil 7ml	115977	
£1.00	Nap Pasta Shells 400g(VE)	160074		£0.69	Cumin Powder 100g	150074		£2.99	Muskaline Perfumed Oil 7ml	115975	
£1.00	Cypressa Cous Cous 500g	079314		£0.79	Turmeric Powder 100g	805465		£2.99	Ghazni Perfumed Oil 7ml	115973	
£1.05	PastanSauce Cheese/Ham&Leek	187226		£0.99	Dried Thyme 40g	189226		£2.99	Ibbi Prayer Perfume 7ml	111926	
£1.00	Economy Mayo (V)	144503		£0.59	Cinnamon Powder 100g	116308		£2.99	Kakool Prayer Perfume 7ml	111928	
£1.00	Econom Salad Cream (V)	200017		£0.85	Mixed Seasoning 100g(VE)	189208		£0.49	Rosaries Beads	137734	
£1.00	Economy Brown Sauce(V)	200018		£0.99	GARI 500g	102365		£0.68	Plain Tooth stick (Miswak)	140398	
£0.69	Economy Ketchup (V)	109463		£0.99	Jerk Seasoning 100g(VE)	189227		£1.11	Prayer Hat (Topi)	098793	
£2.59	Reggae Reggae Sauce	198280		£0.99	Dunns Fish Seasoning 100g	212296			**GENERAL ITEMS**		
£1.99	Heinz Mustard	200047		£1.59	Red Lentils 500g(VE,GF)	193462		£0.49	Toilet Solid Rim Pine	093335	
£1.99	Encona H/Pepper Sauce(VE,H)	073046		£1.09	BlackEye Beans 500g(VE,H,K)	189222		£2.49	Surf Powder Lav/Jas 10Wash	178143	
£1.29	HZ BBQ Sauce	128246		£1.99	Dunns Red Kidney Beans 500g	201074		£2.99	Surf Bio Liquid 560ml	143343	
£1.29	HZ Sweet Chilli Sauce	128248		£1.99	Chapati Flour Medium 1.5kg	188378		£1.99	Lenor Conditioner 22Wash	181714	
£1.19	Sarsons Malt Vinegar	141901		£0.69	Cornmeal Fine 500g(VE,K,H)	189223		£1.00	Economy Non Bio Soap Powder	174552	
£1.49	Soy Sauce 200ml	217894		£0.89	Economy Gravy Granules	128304		£1.00	Economy Fab Conditioner	141975	
£1.49	Heinz Mint Sauce	179816		£1.39	Bisto Gravy Granules	178759		£2.29	Daz Handwash 960g	789743	
£1.99	Mango Chutney (V)	109076		£0.99	Beef Oxo Cubes 6s	601400		£3.73	Bio-D NonBio Wash Pdr(VE)	095775	
£2.43	Spicy Mixed Pickle	111804		£0.99	Chicken Oxo Cubes 6's	601580		£0.60	Washing up Liquid 500ml	192962	
£1.89	Branston Pickle Sq Sml Cnk	203217		£1.35	Veg Oxo Cubes 12s (V)	185386		£1.99	Bio-D Wash Up Lqd (VE)	193428	
£0.99	Mixed Olives (VE)	110647		£0.85	Paxo Sage&On Stuffing(V)	101685		£1.00	All Purpose Cloth 4s	131534	
£0.89	Mugshot Sweet&Sour Pasta(V)	182795		£0.99	Creamed Coconut 200g(VE,GF)	071464		£1.00	Incense Sticks 20s	133658	
£0.89	Mugshot Tom&Herb Pasta(V)	219677		£0.09	Self Raising Flour 1kg	195543		£1.52	Incense Sticks Premium 15s	109359	
£0.59	Cock Soup 50g	189207		£0.89	Plain Flour 1kg	195542		£1.02	Less Smoke Incense Sticks 20s	103587	
£0.99	HZ Tomato Soup 400g(V)	190283		£1.89	Whitworths Dried Fruit 350g	190556		£1.00	Ash Catcher Incense Holder	133656	
£0.75	Economy Ravioli 400g	160102		£1.89	Whitworths Sultanas 325g	190558		£0.50	Gel Air Freshener	145114	
£0.55	Econ Spaghetti Hoops (V)	182375		£0.79	Jif Lemon Squeezy 55ml	365337		£0.95	Toilet Tissue Twin Pack	201595	
£0.95	HZ Baked Beans 415g(V,GF)	266581		£1.25	W/worths Desiccated Coconut	606490		£2.45	Safety Matchstick Cutter	093599	
£0.35	Economy Baked Beans 410g	113633		£0.65	Economy Tomato Puree 200g	128596		£2.45	Plain H/lss Mdl Matches 2000s	093624	
£0.75	Macaroni Cheese (V)	128593		£1.15	Mayloway Curry Sce Mix Hot	097077		£2.15	Wood Glue 110g	094506	
£0.55	Tinned Whole Carrots	103064		£0.99	Spaghetti Bolognese Sac(V)	126512		£0.32	Med Fine Sandpaper Sheet	093623	
£0.55	Tinned Garden Peas	199822		£0.69	Colmans Sauce Mix Cheese	206126		£1.03	Craft Hobby Brush	094781	
£1.00	Mushrooms Button 285g	141647			**SUPPLEMENTS**			£1.29	Alarm Clock(Needs AA Bat)	114383	
£0.65	Red Kidney Beans 400g	180242		£1.15	Nurish Banana 400g(V)	124109		£1.25	Audio Cassette	134227	
£0.40	Economy Chopd Tomatoes 400g	126366		£1.15	Nurish Chocolate 400g(V)	124108		£7.99	Safety Flat Sheet White	124286	
£0.75	Economy New Potatoes 560g	165400		£1.15	Nurish Strawberry 400g	124106		£2.99	Pillowcase White	136547	
£0.75	Economy Sweetcorn Tin 340g	129117		£1.15	Nurish Vanilla 400g(V)	124105		£10.49	Safety Duvet Cover Blue	147137	
£0.55	Sea Chick Peas 400g(VE,GF)	091862		£2.29	Sport Mixer Bottle 500ml	183775		£2.99	Pillowcase Blue	147152	
£0.89	Spinach Leaf 380g(VE,GF)	171394		£6.10	Creatine Mondrate 120g(V)	094723		£10.49	Safety Duvet Cover Lemon	136198	
£5.49	Ackees 540g	404083		£8.67	Elite Protein Banana (V)	094724		£2.99	Pillowcase Lemon	136202	
£0.99	Okra 400g	147489		£8.67	Elite Protein S/berry (V)	094725		£22.99	Safety Sgl Quilt 9 Tog	123996	
£1.00	Pineapple in Juice 432g	188112		£21.57	DP90 Strawberry 750g	184439		£9.99	Safety Single Pillow	124287	
£1.00	Princes S/berrys In Syrup	188113		£19.97	Spectrum Whey Protein 450g	199052		£1.19	Plastic Coated Playing Cards	128317	
£1.00	FCocktail Syrup410g(VE,GF)	188103		£7.75	Only Whey 250g (V)	105827		£3.49	Premium Plastic Can Opener	142525	
£1.00	Pear Halves Juice410g(VE,GF)	188107		£16.37	Only Whey 750g (V)	184435		£20.16	Mwave Food Storer 650ml	139108	
£1.00	Peaches in Juice 410g(VE,GF)	188106		£39.97	Ultimate Mass Bana 3kg(V)	184445		£2.49	CL Food Storer 2.25L	626192	
£0.99	Princes Grapefruit Seg/Juice	110372		£19.99	Creatine Monohydrate Powder 500g	218705		£2.99	Square Clip Containers	203334	
£0.85	Mandarins In Syrup 312g	176706		£21.59	DP90 Chocolate 750g	218703		£0.85	HS Medium Food/Frzr Bag	121746	
£1.69	Cherry Pie Filling 410g	136680		£44.99	Titan Mass Complete 1.2kg	218402		£1.00	Roasting Bag 12pk	201492	

You will be limited to the amount of money you can spend each week which is linked to your IEP status.

Catalogue Spends

As you progress through your sentence there is also a catalogue purchase system, these are approved companies that supply approved items that can be purchased and added to your prop card.

PlayStation and Xbox consoles can be purchased but they are models that are unable to connect to the internet so don't expect modern versions or modern games.

You can also purchase books from approved suppliers if what you want is not available in the library.

Contact with the outside world

Letters will become an integral part of your life in prison, not only does writing them pass the time, but you also find the replies a comfort and an important way of keeping in touch with loved ones.

The prison normally allows you to have 1 outgoing letter per week where they will supply the paper, envelope and stamp/postage.

However, more proficient writers can purchase additional stationery and stamps via their canteen sheets.

Letters to be posted out will be taken to the wing office, they must not be sealed as all post will be checked coming in and going out.

The only exception to this is rule 39, this is a legal privilege letter that can only be used between you and your legal team and an officer will normally check before sealing it that is a genuine letter to your legal team.

As mentioned, all incoming mail will be opened and checked by prison staff. The exception again is post that is covered by Rule 39, your legal team will label the post accordingly and this should arrive at your cell unopened.

At the time of writing this book, there was no procedure in place for prisoners to send e-mails although it is being discussed.

There is, in certain prisons, the function to e-mail a prisoner - this is printed and delivered in the same way as conventional mail but is quicker to send in than traditional mail.

To check if your prison has this facility go to www.emailaprisoner.com for details.

The other way to keep in contact with people on the outside is by using prison phones.

During your induction, you were given a personal PIN, every single number you want to call has to be registered, checked and approved.

All prison calls are monitored and recorded, charges can be brought against you for things discussed and the calls used as evidence in court.

Again, the exception to this are calls to your legal team, the number will be registered as such and these calls are not allowed to be monitored.

They will check the number you say is your legal team is actually your legal team.

First VO (Visiting Order)

A VO is a visiting order, no one can visit the prison without one of these being filled out and accepted by the prison.

It is a form of app that indicates your relationship with the person, their name, address, age and any other important information.

Each visitor will be screened by the prison before them accepting the visit, this is done to ensure that no rules or bail conditions are being broken by you having contact.

You will be allowed up to 5 people on a visit (normally 2 adults and 3 children).

Your first VO will be given to you at your induction to fill out.

Moving forward you will need to complete a VO for every single visit you want to have, so it is a process you will need to get familiar with.

Pitfalls - What to avoid

Moving on to your first wing can present you with all kinds of challenges and temptations.

It is easy to get caught up with the wrong people because new arrivals become a target for seasoned prisoners either as potential customers or as workers.

The biggest and most important bit of advice we can give is to not get involved with drugs.

Pretty much every drug is available inside prison but to give you an idea we have listed some of the most prevalent:

- Spice (synthetic cannabis - hallucinogenic)
- Heroin
- Crack
- Cannabis
- Cocaine
- MDMA/ecstasy
- Speed
- Subutex (an opioid used for heroin addiction)

These pale into insignificance when you take into consideration the cottage industry in prescription drugs given out by the prison healthcare departments.

This becomes evident when you look at the medicine hatch at any given time, in any given prison in the UK estate as the queue's only get longer and the amount of prescribed medication is given out like confetti.

As with everything in prison, even medicine is a tradable commodity and the market is more active than any other.

Healthcare staff in prison do a wonderful job dealing with complex mental health issues and working in challenging environments.

However, the privatisation of the healthcare departments within the prison estate, means they are targeted by shareholders on the number of drugs they give out because that is where the money is made.

So, there is a direct correlation between privatisation and the increase in prescribed medication throughout the prison system and this has fed into a thriving illegal economy of misery and addiction on every wing up and down the country.

The next thing to avoid is borrowing anything. If we take for example a mobile phone, these are illegal in prison but there will be a number of them on every single wing.

It can be tempting to pay to use one for one call, we understand the desire to be in contact with the outside world but ultimately that one call can lead to a big problem.

If security ever finds the phone then they will search through the historical data to find which numbers were called. If this can be linked to you through your contacts list then you will end up on an IEP or adjudication and highly likely that you will be denied phone privileges and visits for some time.

You are also likely to lose your enhanced status and have a negative entry put on to your prison record which will impact you later on in your sentence.

People will ask you to store/hide items for them, as a new arrival it will be considered that you are less likely to have a cell search.

However, this is not the case anyone can be selected for a search and no reason needs to be given.

Being found with drugs, knives, stolen items, electrical equipment and phones will be determined as being yours if it is in your cell with your belongings.

The reason that most people allow this to happen is that they are trying to endear themselves to their new peers but the reality is that this act of bravado, to make yourself look like one of the boys does little to ingratiate you amongst them as they are using you as a patsy (mug).

Work and Education

Unfortunately, due to the way the prison system works, you will earn more money for doing menial jobs than you will for education but this is a short-sighted way of looking at it but understandable.

If your education is limited we strongly advise that you take the opportunity whilst you are in prison to attempt to address this.

The one thing you have in abundance in prison is time, using this time to address educational issues will serve you well on release.

It is also vital that we highlight the fact a poor education or the inability to read or write is absolutely nothing to be ashamed of or fear.

Terry had dyslexia and became a best-selling author and a GHQ magazine feature writer on his release from prison.

There is plenty of help available, but you will need to take ownership and responsibility for the fact you have issues you wish to address and seek out the help required.

Each year there are 1000's of men that enter prison with little or no education, they can't read or write and often isolate themselves in their cell or disrupt classrooms because they believe admitting they can't do something will lead to ridicule.

The reality from our experience is that once an issue has been highlighted, prisoners tend to be supportive and will help address the problem.

Peer-led support programs are something that should be celebrated inside most prisons and encouraged more, the reality is people on the outside hear little about this positive support network run by prisoners for prisoners.

If you are well educated and can read and write, being part of a peer-led support group helping those that can't is an excellent way to pass time and will look good on your prison record moving forward.

This is also a way of helping change someone's life for the better and is an incredibly rewarding experience for both parties, which is hard to come by especially in prison.

Education

The prison education courses are somewhat limited and the level you can attain is very much entry-level stuff. However, they offer a good base and can provide some very useful skills depending on what you want to do post-release.

For people who have little to no education then prison education is an excellent way to get some qualifications.

The biggest problem with prison courses is that the wrong people access them. You tend to find those with a good education already will enrol on courses because they prefer to be in a classroom than out cleaning a wing or sweating in a kitchen.

The prison won't stop this because having people on courses that they know will pass them looks good in their stats, so it benefits them in the long run.

The flip side of that is that people who need the education are often too embarrassed to admit that and are more comfortable cleaning the wings or working in the kitchens.

Depending on the prison you will find that there is a diverse range of courses on offer across the estate and some funding options are in place for more complex courses with people like the Prisoner's Education Trust (PET).

Every prison will offer English and Math's courses, there is a minimum level that people are expected to attain in these two subjects and you will have to complete this regardless.

Below is a list of some of the examples of courses and subjects that are on offer, this is not a comprehensive list and as you will see there are vocational and non-vocational courses on offer:

- Visual Arts - Drawing, painting.
- Horticulture
- Hospitality and Catering
- Health and Social Care
- Languages
- Agriculture
- Construction
- Counselling and Mentoring
- Plumbing
- Animal Care
- Health and Beauty
- Beekeeping
- Business Skills
- Bookkeeping
- Sports and Fitness

- Road Haulage
- Rail track
- Forklift

It is very easy to stay in your comfort zone and stick to what you know but it is important to challenge yourself and using the time in prison to gain new skills and qualifications will be far more rewarding than simply doing a wing cleaning job.

Work

Work inside prison is better paid than education and for this reason, it is more appealing to a lot of people. Don't expect to be on minimum wage or earn serious money - Education pays around £9 per week and certain jobs will pay anywhere from £7.50 up to £40 a week (£40 is rare and depends on the outside provider).

So, you are not going to be quid's in by any stretch of the imagination but you will be able to purchase a few luxuries to make life a little more bearable.

We will say it again though, don't let the short-sighted attitude of money now cloud the bigger picture, working in the warehouse, kitchen or scrubbing a wing floor is not going to help you when you leave, so our advice is to learn a new skill or qualification that might help you once you have left prison.

Generally, the jobs around prison involve helping the prison function in some way, you have orderlies that help run induction, library, chapel, peer mentors etc.

Then you have jobs that focus on cleaning areas of the prison, jobs in the kitchen to prepare and serve food, laundry services and jobs to maintain the grounds of the prison.

Finally, some prisons will have outside agencies that produce or manufacture things on prison grounds, car number plates for example at some prisons in the UK.

DHL also run their canteen delivery and supply business for prisons inside prisons.

Whether you decide to do education or work, it will form an important part of your life and is crucial in getting time out of your cell.

Learning to read

As we have said numerous times already not being able to read is nothing to be ashamed of and we completely understand that this can be a source of embarrassment but it doesn't have to be.

If someone is currently reading this to you then please be reassured that there is plenty of help on offer in prison to address this.

Each year thousands of men learn to read whilst in prison which opens up a whole host of employment opportunities on release.

Most prisons use the Shannon Trust reading plan to help, this is an interactive way for someone to learn supported by a fellow prisoner who can read.

Shannon Trust train their mentors and they follow a set plan to help you read:

- You will meet up to 5 times a week
- Meetings will be 20 minutes
- You learn at your own pace, there are no exams
- Sessions are one to one and held in private
- The learning material is written for adult learners so you won't be reading children's books

Some of the other benefits of learning to read include; making it easier to keep in touch with friends and family, ordering canteen, filling out prison apps, reading legal correspondence and making the most of the education on offer.

Distance learning - Open University

For the more educated and those on longer sentences there is an option to do something called distance learning.

This is a way to complete a degree or higher education course and can be a good way to set yourself up for the future.

You will need to either fund or find funding for the course yourself but there are funding providers available and the prison will have a list of these available.

If this is something you are interested in please speak to the prison as soon as possible and you can start to get the information and making funding requests.

Occupying your time (this is something you have plenty of)

Finding ways to consume time in prison becomes a never-ending battle and a lot of people will fall into the trap of self-medicating to pass the time being high.

Boredom plays a huge role in why people offend and re-offend, so this is one of the biggest lessons you can learn in prison - how to manage it.

Boredom is also one of the biggest contributing factors in drug use in and out of prison, so learning to cope with it can have far-reaching benefits.

We will cover the main things the prison offers to get you out of your cell and off the wing. A lot of men will find a hobby in prison-like making matchstick models of things.

Reading is a hugely popular past-time and as Terry demonstrated writing is a way to release emotions, it is cathartic and a great way to pass time.

Exercise

You should be given at least 30-minutes of outdoor time each day, going into the yard and walking around is a good way to let off steam and escape the monotony of the wing.

You can also exercise and run in the yard and some prisons will make time available for you to take part in football if the facilities and weather allow.

Cell routines are also a viable option to keep yourself mentally fit and healthy.

An example of some of the exercises you can do in your cell are as follows:

- Step-ups on a chair
- Push-ups
- Squats
- Burpees
- Star jumps
- Sit-ups

A fun way of doing a cell workout is doing something called the card workout. Lay out six random cards facing upwards, the number of the card is the number of the reps you do - so card 1 is step-ups - 10 of clubs = 10 step-ups.

Card 2 would be push-ups - 4 of hearts = 4 push-ups.

And follow this until you have gone through the whole pack of 52 cards, as you get fitter and the card deck becomes easier you can start to either double the number of reps per card or go through the pack a second time. This is a good barometer of improvement.

Good luck.

Association/free time

Association time will vary depending on regime and prison, the time of day you get this will also vary but you should get time out of your cell every day.

During this time, you may decide to get a shower or bath, most regimes will have separate shower times built into the timetable but you may decide to either stay in bed when this happens or have missed it for another reason, so association is a good time to take one.

Association is the time where you can clean your cell, visit the wing office for applications, play pool, play table tennis, use the phones or speak to other people on the wing.

Your wing may have a TV room and board games too.

Some wings even have one or two exercise bikes that can be used during association if you are an enhanced prisoner.

This is also a good time to use the toilet for more solid deposits without anyone watching you or being offended by what is happening.

Whilst that may sound trivial you would be surprised at how many people struggle with going to the toilet in front of someone, association becomes one of the few times you can manage to go.

It isn't uncommon for new prisoners to suffer from constipation in the first few weeks, bathroom privacy is something everyone takes for granted and something after you are released that you will cherish more but also the lack of it can contribute to problems as you adjust to your new life.

Gym

Prison gyms are one of the most used facilities in most prisons.

To attend the prison gym, you will need to have completed the induction and then you have to fill out an app (by now I am sure you can see that apps are everywhere and an essential part of the prison system) to request your gym hours.

Once you have filled out your app, you will be allocated gym time, this will depend on your IEP status as to how much time you will get.

If you miss your gym slot and you have not informed the gym beforehand (for example a medical appointment) you will lose your gym time moving forward and will need to reapply.

Faith

Prisons will cater for every faith and will make reasonable efforts to ensure that your religious needs are met.

A lot of men rediscover faith whilst in prison but some attend simply for a biscuit and a chat.

Attending a faith service is another way to get out of your cell and off the wing, the moral lessons being taught are often something you will find yourself connecting with more after your freedom has been removed.

You will also find yourself praying for a lot more in prison - You will pray to go home, for your family and not to get beat up.

But the most commonly used prayer is definitely "Please release me, I will never commit a crime again"

It probably won't surprise you to learn that to attend a faith service you will need to fill out an app.

This will differ from prison to prison and some will have evolved to simply having a list but you will need a pen regardless.

Library

The library is normally a nice and quiet refuge in most prisons you need to request a library visit by using an app but going to the library is a good way to waste an hour and enjoy a quieter area of the prison.

Prison libraries are normally well-stocked with a broad range of books, you can request books and providing it is available in a prison library somewhere in the prison estate they can request it be sent for you.

A book that we can highly recommend is Grendon's Therapy - The Inside Story by Terry Ellis.

The library is another tool you can use to escape your cell and the wing, we can't stress enough how valuable this becomes in dealing with your sentence.

Examples of Prisoner Art

If you are going to be spending some significant time residing at Her Majesty's pleasure then learning a new skill is a great way to occupy your time.

A very good friend of ours did just that, Craig Ball. He took up art and he is superb, famous inmates such as Charles Salvador (formerly Charles Bronson) have also become excellent artists during their time in prison.

Here is a very small collection of Craig's artwork which can be viewed on Instagram by searching for @itsmecraigball.

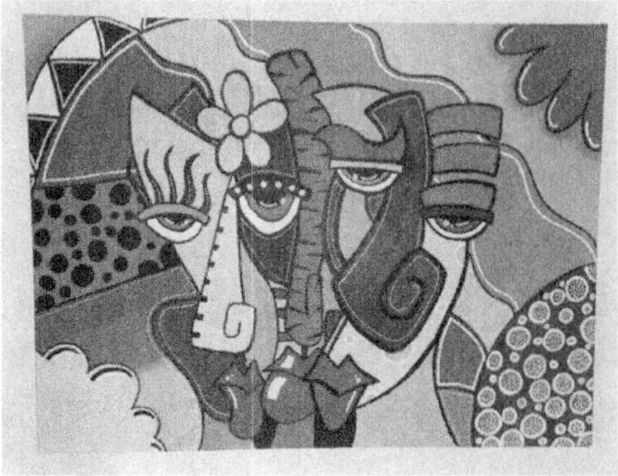

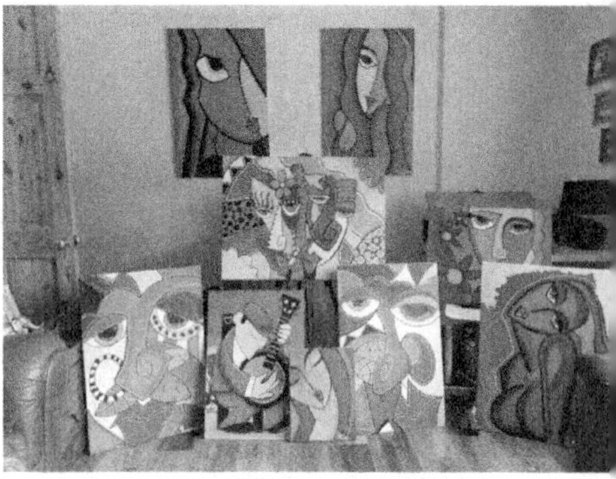

Information for families

The following section is aimed to give families the little bits of information that are foreign to first-time prisoners and their loved ones and tie together all the many different segments of detail that are relevant to families who have someone in or facing prison.

A common criticism of the prison service is that they don't communicate properly with families and that they often don't present information in the easiest way.

Whilst we accept that this is true, we must highlight the fact that at any given time there are around 90,000 prisoners in England and Wales. Given that there are such large numbers to deal with it is unreasonable to expect that personalised responses are practical.

Hopefully, you will find the information covered in this section and the book as a whole will provide you with any information either missed or not readily available.

Visits

First and foremost, there can be no visits without an approved visiting order (V.O). This will be filled out by the prisoner and once accepted you will receive a notification.

You **MUST** bring this with you on the visit, even though the prison will have a record that you are visiting you have to bring it with you or you will be refused entry.

Along with your visiting order, everyone on the order will need to bring an ID to prove they are the person listed on the V.O.

Acceptable forms of ID are as follows:

- Driving License
- Passport
- Employer or Student ID (with photo)
- Inland revenue registration card
- Senior citizen public transport card (with photo)

If you don't have any of the above photo ID then the prison may accept two of the following (we recommend checking with the prison beforehand).

- Birth or marriage certificate
- A benefit card
- A rail or bus pass (with photo)
- A cheque book or debit card
- A trade union or National Union of Students (NUS) card
- A young person proof of age card
- A rent book and statement
- A tenancy agreement

Children between the ages of 10 years and 17 years will also require ID and that can be one of the following:

- A family passport
- A birth certificate
- Medical card
- Travelcard with photograph
- A student photo ID

A birth certificate will be sufficient for children under the age of 10 years old, a replacement or copy can be obtained from the registry office in the town of birth for a small fee if required.

All visitors must be prepared to be searched and it is a common procedure to have sniffer dogs walk the visits queue. It is an illegal offence to try and smuggle anything into the prison, if you are suspected of carrying anything the prison officers have the power to detain you on-site and will notify the police.

You will not be allowed any mobile phones, bags or personal items into the visiting hall. For this reason, we advise taking a few pound coins to the visit with you, you will need to put any excess belongings into lockers - the prison estate is updating lockers to pin access lockers which are free but a large section of the prisons will still use £1 coins.

There will be a snack shop in the visiting hall, the prison rules about money in visits vary - some will allow a small amount of cash (£20) to be taken in for use at the shop, others will not allow any cash and you will exchange money for vouchers before you go in.

It is important to check the prison specific rules before you go.

Prisons do make efforts to ensure that the visiting areas are welcoming and as "un" prisonlike as possible, they pay particular attention to this on family days but there are areas of the prison that are intimidating on your first time there.

Family days are, as the name suggests days for the family, in particular younger family members. They are reserved for standard and enhanced prisoners and they are held in a more relaxed environment with things like face painting and activities on offer.

These are popular when they come around and are often oversubscribed, therefore if you have the opportunity to attend one make the effort to attend as non-attendance will have taken the spot from another family.

On rare occasions, you may arrive at the prison for a visit and find the visit has been cancelled. The prison will try to make the effort to inform people ahead of time but sometimes they are unable to reach the necessary people.

A visit cancellation will normally happen due to a behavioural issue with the person you are visiting. As frustrating as it is for you, the prison will not change their mind, no matter how many times or how loudly you demand to speak to the Governor.

Our advice to prisoners is that if you know you have a visit booked, be on your best behaviour in the week leading up to it and make sure you don't give an officer any excuse to take it away from you.

Post

Post is one of the main ways of keeping in contact with inmates, what seems like a short letter not containing very much information to you, is something the person in prison looks forward to.

The prisoner may tell you they don't need constant letters from people, most sit and wait for their mail each day and look forward to it with excitement, whether they care to admit it or not.

You do not need to share personal information in letters, remember prison staff check every single one but regular contact is always appreciated.

When writing to a prisoner you will need their prison number, wing and cell location (if possible), name, prison address and postcode. You also need to write on the back of the envelope the sender's details.

Sending in money

First and foremost, sending in cash to prison is not safe nor recommended. Whilst you can send it, there is no record of you sending it and there is every chance it will never make it into the spends account for the person you sent it to.

Postal orders have been the go-to method of sending in money for years, they can be sent in with your regular letters and will be processed when the mail is checked by security.

They will need to be made out to NOMS Agency with the prisoner's name and prison number on the back, as an added form of security you can mention it in the letter that there is a postal order enclosed and the value of that order. This will give the inmate something they can chase up should it not appear in their spending account.

Cheques are the other thing that for years was considered a safe bet, exactly the same process as postal orders for these, payable to NOMS Agency with the prisoner name and number on the back of the cheque.

Cheques take longer to process because the prison needs to wait for the funds to clear before releasing them to the prisoner's spending account.

As prisons move with the times and only about 20 years after internet banking became a thing, some prisons now have the facilities to accept money electronically. After a few months in prison, you will realise what an incredible watershed moment this is.

You will need the prisoner name, number and date of birth.

The public prison estate uses a separate system from the private-run prisons (G4S, Serco, etc.) because it would be too easy for people if there was only one site.

So, for the public sector prisons, you will go to www.gov.uk/send-prisoner-money and for the private-run prisons you will go to secure-payment-services.com/index.cfm

Currently, the list of private prisons using this service are:

- Addiewell
- Altcourse
- Ashfield
- Bronzefield
- Doncaster
- Dovegate
- Forest Bank
- Kilmarnock
- Lowdham Grange
- Northumberland
- Oakwood
- Parc

- Peterborough
- Rye Hill
- Thameside
- Yarls Wood IRC

Leave a message

In the last few years, there has been a concerted effort by prisons to make life a little easier for friends, family and loved ones to stay in contact.

The systems in place are by no means perfect but compared to what was on offer, it is a step in the right direction.

Previously contact could be made difficult because the only real-time phones that could be used was during association. As you're not in prison you probably don't realise that this can mean 30 to 40 prisoners on a wing spur all trying to use 6 phones in 30 minutes of association time - chaos.

Add into that the fact that association could be at 2.30 pm and you work until 5 pm and you can see why a phone call could prove problematic.

So, the prisons have introduced a voice mail function - you sign up at www.prisonvoicemail.com, they have a range of packages on offer, the prisoner gets a phone number to call from the prison to retrieve messages and can leave a reply.

It enables you to leave messages anytime and the prisoner can pick them up and reply when they have the opportunity to use a phone.

The cost to the prisoner is the same as a call to a landline (around 8p per minute), which is cheaper than if they rang a mobile phone.

The service runs via an app on your phone, this will notify you when the prisoner dials into your voice message and allow you to join the call live, this works out cheaper for the prisoner than calling your mobile directly.

This is a welcome upgrade with the prison phone system and whilst we don't have a great deal to praise prisons with this is certainly a huge positive.

Research for inmates

This section could also be titled "stating the obvious" to anyone that has been through the prison system however, when we spoke to families it surprised us how many people didn't realise there is no WI-FI or internet in prison.

So, with that in mind, we should say that there is no internet in prison. Well, no legal internet in prison, there is an increasing number of illegal smartphones in prisons but for argument's sake, let's assume that your loved one is not doing anything they shouldn't be.

This is a very important point because we take the Internet for granted and it is our first port of call when we want to research anything.

This is where you come in.

Depending on the length of the sentence there are a whole host of things an inmate may need your assistance with and your googling skills can be put to the test.

If, for example, your inmate would like to do a course in prison that requires funding, they will probably require you to do the donkey work and see what funders are available in their prison's area.

You may also need to do legal research for them if they plan to appeal their sentence or are on remand awaiting trial.

You won't be able to pass on information about fellow prisoners or the blueprints for the prison but reasonable research about courses or legal matters will be allowed through the prison mail system.

Help with visits

Not every prison is conveniently situated on the west coast mainline or right next to a bus station, in fact, some are in the middle of nowhere.

If your loved one happens to be in a prison that falls into the middle of nowhere category then our advice is to check with the prison directly about getting there, if you need to use public transport.

As we stated earlier visits are important and with that in mind some prisons will run minibuses for visits from the local town centre if there is not a reliable and regular public transport system close by.

Not everyone will be able to afford to travel to and from prison but that doesn't mean it isn't possible, if you are over 18 and the visit is to a close family member or partner there may be financial assistance available.

If you receive certain benefits then you may be able to get assistance to visit someone. For this, you are about to get a taste of life inside because you are going to have to fill out an app.

The benefits that qualify for the help are:

- Universal credit
- Income Support
- Income-based jobseekers allowance
- Employment and support allowance (ESA)
- Tax credits
- Pension credit

You will need to speak to the assisted prison visits unit, we provide the details below and you will need to complete the relevant forms. They come with guidance but you can also request help with filling them out if you require them.

Assisted Prison Visits Unit
assisted.prison.visits@noms.gsi.gov.uk
Tel: 0300 063 2100
Monday to Friday 9 am to 5 pm

Assisted Prison Visits Unit
PO Box 2152
Birmingham
B15 1SD

Vulnerable Prisoners - Family Support

Again, we approached Joe Chapman for this section of the book, his expertise in this area and ongoing support for families in this particular was something we couldn't simply miss.

We are so fortunate to have been able to call on someone with so much information and knowledge in this area.

UNLIKELY ANGELS

(The story of two women in crisis – Emma and Rosie)

"Family isn't always blood. It's the people in your life who want you in theirs. The ones who accept you for who you are. The ones who would do anything to see you smile and who love you no matter what". Anon.

You could be sat at work, picking the kids up from school, sat enjoying a glass of wine, be told over dinner, find out through social media or get a call from either a police officer or your loved one from the police station. But when you get the news that your loved one has been accused of a sexual offence prepare yourself for the life you know to be very different from now on.......

Emma found out via two scribbled notes that had been left in her letterbox from a police officer asking her to contact them in relation to an incident concerning her partner. At first, she thought that he had died, in a car crash going to work that morning. She was already anxious as she had not heard from him all day and he hadn't responded to the 3 messages she'd sent, most unlike him. Emma said "Sick rising in my throat I called the number, the officer answered immediately and then boom, she just came out with it "Your partner has been in custody all day, he was arrested in connection to a serious sexual assault, we just need to ask you a few questions" I immediately vomited."

Families of sexual offenders are, without doubt, punished deeply for a crime they never committed. There has to be an understanding in any civilised society of the suffering that these families face through no fault of their own.

Similarly, a lady called Rosie recalls "I have been married to my husband for over 40 years and we have a grown-up son and daughter.

Up until the point of my husband's arrest, I thought, rather smugly, that we had a small but pretty amazing, close family. That changed in a heartbeat when we got that early morning knock on the front door. My world fell apart as the man I loved with every fibre of my being admitted to cases of historic sexual abuse. I felt as though I entered a parallel universe, my heart was broken beyond words and my head was barely habitable. This state became the new norm for me during the following 11 months that my husband was under investigation by the police."

Peoples experiences during investigations vary greatly.

Emma says the police asked, "Do you live together?" I replied "Yes."

"Are you having a sexual relationship?"

"Well yes but it's not like that, I think that you should come to my home to discuss it."

"And they did just that, two female officers one a constable the other a sergeant sat in my lounge and after ascertaining the facts surrounding the open nature of our relationship, and writing my comments down they drew the meeting to a close by making threats that social services would be called should I speak with my partner.

And that was it, I didn't lay eyes on the two officers again until the first day of his trial. Both of them dressed more for a day at the races than a 3-day court hearing which would change our world forever. They acknowledged who I was but besides that first nod, eye contact was not made again until he was found guilty."

For Rosie, the waiting to go to trial was horrendous. Apart from telling a few close friends, they had to pretend that everything was normal; but nothing was normal.

"This period of limbo is torture. The not knowing. Wondering what the sentence might be. Wondering how many friends I would lose, would it affect my work, how would people react? We do, after all, live in a society that emphasises sensationalism, revenge, and gossip."

Exchanging pleasantries with people in the street was a strain. 'Hi, how are you?'

'Oh, fine thanks; yes, everything's great.'

"When inside I wanted to say I am hurting so bad I need morphine and my husband is dying of grief and remorse. How's your day?'

But instead, we put on brave faces."

Emma supported her partner at court, and she described how the police officers sat directly in front of her throughout the whole trial, and for the most part, she was the only support that he had. She cannot recommend strongly enough that anyone in that situation has someone sat beside them. "It is a truly harrowing experience listening to the evidence and seeing your loved one sat in the dock."

Take notice of the rules and etiquette expected of you during the proceedings, if you wish to be excused from the court a small nod of the head facing the judge before you exit, not having your mobile phone in view regardless of it being switched on or not, and probably most importantly your protests and outbursts will not ever assist the situation. Stay classy at all times.

Rosie faced her worst fears in court.

"After 11 seemingly endless months of investigation, my husband received a lengthy prison sentence along with a diagnosis of prostate cancer just a few days before his conviction. My heart and soul were lacerated by grief too great to describe. It was at that moment that my sentence began.

And then it came out in the press. At this point, you may be wondering why I was standing by my husband. It would, after all, have been so very much easier to walk away.

Briefly, the reason is that I have known him for a very long time, and I have seen all the astonishing good he has done in his life. I refused to throw all that away. And there are always many complex reasons why a good man does something very wrong, and it isn't because he has suddenly become bad. Loving one person hard, and long, and well can be one of the most difficult and yet rewarding things to do. And if you knew my husband, you would understand.

The media had a field day. It was in the local press and the Metro magazine on every bus and train, etc., across the country. It was also on local radio and television. The media tells half the story, twists and exaggerate the facts and incites hatred. I don't understand why it is even legal.

And my husband, at this point, is safely out of the firing line. I am bearing the full brunt of it."

Emma describes the process following the delivery of a guilty verdict.

"If your loved one has not been taken to court from a prison prepare yourself for them to be remanded into custody immediately, should the verdict be guilty. Having a bag prepared is an absolute must. "Seeing my partner dressed in expensive suit trousers, a prison-issue sweatshirt and a pair of black school pumps only encouraged me in thanking him for not telling me it was fancy dress, I'd have made an effort had I known. Whilst it did have us laugh briefly, no one benefits from not having taken a bag to the court, just in case."

The shock of a guilty verdict is something I don't think anyone can prepare for. In her case, the word sounded alien and it wasn't spoken, it was bellowed, in her face. The prosecution barrister turned to her and mouthed an apology. The officers remained sat in front of her. She just sat there, stunned.

Due to the severity of the offences he was remanded immediately into custody, they touched hands via the glass surrounding the dock and then he was taken away. His barrister immediately vanished and that was that. The following morning she located the prison to which he had been sent and booked a visit for the following day which was Christmas eve; at that point, she took his clothes into the prison for him but he didn't receive them for over a week."

Meanwhile, Rosie was coming to terms with life without her husband.

She received anonymous letters and a vigilante Facebook page that said when they found the house, they would burn it down.

She was lucky as she had no small children at home, but that is a truly dreadful situation that many, women, and men find themselves in as they struggle to keep their children safe.

"Fortunately, a lot of neighbours were kind and I am very lucky. This is largely because my husband had gone round to them beforehand and said, this is what I have done, I am going to go to prison, and I would like you to look after my wife. That took huge courage. But this is the kind of man he is."

Many others took a different view. Some decided that because she was standing by her husband, she must have known.

"Oh, how that particular comment hurts. I have tortured myself with the thoughts 'Why didn't I know? Could I have done something differently? Could I have stopped this? Could I have prevented so much pain to victims, victims' families, our family…?' But of course, it wasn't even on my radar. Those committing these sorts of crimes even hide it from themselves."

But it is the pub talk and village gossip that can be so cruel. At one point, it was even decided that she should be investigated too. It blew over, as things do, but it was a hard and lonely time when she was dealing with immense, unspeakable grief and learning to live on her own for the first time in her life.

She reflects, "My daughter, whom I had always considered to be my best friend had chosen to leave the family and have nothing more to do with us. I accept that it was all too much for her but grieving for my husband and grieving for my daughter was a double blow and felt like bereavement without ever having a funeral.

I am grateful beyond words that my incredible son and his amazing partner remained unflinchingly loyal throughout."

Financially things were hard. And again, she was the one to be affected. She had lost her husband's income, but every prisoner of pensionable age has their state pension stopped as well. She had some health issues that mean she can only work part-time, but paying the bills was now totally down to her.

"I feel very strongly that stopping the state pension is cruel. The majority of people in prison are men. There are increasingly older men in prison, which means that there are a huge number of older women who are being financially punished for something they didn't do."

Her bank got wind of the offences and closed their account without warning. She also found that their home insurance was invalid. Insurers are not keen on ensuring the homes of those convicted of sexual offences, apparently because of the possibility of vigilante attack. This knowledge didn't help her sleep at night. Insurance was offered at four times the previous premium.

It is also possible that she will have to move. Because she is standing by her husband, her future is uncertain. It is possible that her husband will not be able to come back to live in this house because of its location. She would like to know, as this deeply affects her future. The probation service could advise. But after a year of her husband's repeated efforts to contact them, there has been no response.

So, for the next 'X' number of years, Rosie's life is about balancing work and looking after the house and her health, surviving birthdays, Christmas, and social media, and visiting her husband in prison.

Emma describes her first prison experience.

"I'd like to think I'm a pretty strong person but having never visited anyone in prison before it destroyed me. I suffered a panic attack, the security checks, the volume of people, most of which were visiting mains prisoners and I was certain they knew that I wasn't. In all the time that he was in Forest Bank, I always assumed that they sat us at the point nearest the exits due to my funny episode on that first visit. That is not the case in a mains prison."

Vulnerable prisoners are sat there to protect them, should another inmate decide to attack them, it happens, and she witnessed it first-hand.

And the potential to be attacked is also a reality in the community. Media intrusion and having what feels like the world judge you and your loved one, is by far one of the hardest challenges, post-conviction. Whilst it is accepted that the administration of justice should be carried out in public, in cases where identifying the defendant could jeopardise the lifelong anonymity of the complainant, an automatic reporting restriction order will be made by the judge. If that is not the case this means that for many families, media intrusion will affect them personally.

A member of the press is likely to show their face in the courtroom at some point. They are not difficult to spot and will usually be sat in an area of the courtroom which is specifically for them. They are highly unlikely to try and speak to you and you certainly do not have to engage with them. Due to the internet and the speed at which news stories find their way onto social media, any reports will usually present themselves within 24 hrs.

Some cases are never printed, perhaps praying for a huge news story around the time of your case could hold some merit?

"Nothing can prepare anyone for that moment you first clap eyes on a photo of your loved one with a shock factor headline that will no doubt accompany it. "evil rapist" "sick paedophile". The person that they are talking about is someone that you will most likely never have met. They are not the person that you have allowed to share your life with. Acknowledging those words and whom they are discussing is a huge hurdle for most of us."

We live in a time where millions of readers are exposed to horror stories daily and as such this has become the "norm" and media intrusion comes in many forms. 'Fly on the wall' documentaries following sex offenders are commonplace these days. Imagine being the partner of someone accused of a "date rape". Invited to the complainant's home, have a bit of sex behind your partners back and then be accused of rape.

Understanding why someone would wish to support their partner after such a disrespectful act is for most, unfathomable. But every day couples forgive infidelity and move on with their lives together. Having an allegation of such magnitude made against your partner, one could argue, would only fuel the desire to separate. Even more so in the attempt to avoid the association your friends, family and colleagues will make once the story is covered in the press.

Emma says "I am a testimony to the fact that no amount of begging, pleading, crying or even threats of harm will prevent any story deemed to be in the public's interest from being either broadcast or published. But ensuring that the safety of yourself and your family is of utmost importance during the first few days and weeks after conviction. I have argued many times that those of us left at home to pick up the pieces are incredibly vulnerable during this time. The police will offer safeguarding advice should you require this and will place a vulnerable marker on your property which will action a first response alert should any reports be made to them. You can report any malicious communications to the police, and they will investigate these.

The best practice is to simply avoid all social media, take time to grieve and accept this new way of life. Neighbours will gossip, curtains will twitch, and you will be judged by many but to coin a great phrase "today's front-page news is tomorrow's chip wrappers".

Rosie has learned a thing or two over this past year of being a prison widow. And she says, "Evenings are a dangerous time, so have a plan. Learn to keep yourself company. There comes a point where you have to re-enter society and risk rejection. Other people's negative reactions say so very much about them and absolutely nothing about you. If someone has had a truly dreadful time and their life has imploded, don't cross the road in embarrassment because you don't know what to say. Just look them in the eye, smile and say hello. It means a lot.

On the other hand, don't try to fix them. Avoid platitudes at all costs.

Don't say "There's a light at the end of the tunnel" Unless you have fully referenced, scientific evidence of this, I'm not interested.

"It's going to get better, I promise." Unless you are my actual fairy godmother, I don't want to hear this.

Back to prison visits. These involve a huge outlay emotionally, physically, and financially. I visit once every three weeks, which amounts to 17 visits per year. Each visit is two hours. This amounts to 34 hours of visit which is approx. one and a half days per year. To see my husband for one and a half days per year, I will drive 3.5 thousand miles. I will spend at least 34 hours in a waiting room. At a conservative estimate, I will spend 1000 hours driving."

In those prison visit waiting rooms and in the support groups that have found their way onto Facebook you will find others just like you, none of us are alone on this journey and you will find yourself in the company of "unlikely angels" who are simply going to be there for you because you matter and the ambition to support one and other is incredibly strong.

The decision to stand by a loved one convicted of a sexual offence is most likely one of the most difficult decisions a person will ever make in their life. As an unseen victim of another's offending life is incredibly difficult at times but it also has its rewarding moments.

Rosie describes her journey to date.

"Booking prison visits. Now there's a thing... Anyone who regularly has to do this will tell you that the system has been brilliantly designed to produce maximum stress. You can do it online; they prefer you to do this. You have to give three options and often wait several days to find out which day you have got. This system is not always reliable, and I have on several occasions seen visitors turned away from the prison because the system hasn't been efficient enough to let the prison know and then you will not be allowed in.

I have seen a mother and three young children turned away from the prison (which is in the South) after they had travelled from Leeds. She had brought her confirmation email with her; it wasn't her fault at all, but she was turned away. She was crying, the children were crying. It was awful.

I am told it is safer to ring the booking line at the prison. It is open from 10 am to 1 pm and you usually have to wait for ages - and I have waited over an hour - before you can get through. You are not in a queue; you just have to keep pressing 'redial' until someone answers or your finger wears out.

I also suffered greatly over my lack of involvement with my husband's treatment for cancer. We have looked after each other when unwell for our whole adult life. Neither of us could be told when his operation was going to be in case, we planned his escape. For many weeks we wondered 'Will it be today?' 'Will the prison remember to take him to the hospital?' They had already messed up several appointments. He had a 5-hour operation and was returned to a filthy prison less than 24 hours afterwards, in pain, catheterised and yet still double handcuffed to two prison officers. This hurts my heart.

His cellmate - a very young man on remand for violent crimes - was an angel. It is not easy in a tiny cell with no privacy, with a catheter and then extreme incontinence and limited access to laundry but with this young man's gentleness and care, my husband made a full recovery. It still distresses me that I couldn't be there for him, but I will be grateful to that young man forever.

When you have loved someone for a very long time, you tend to be in tune with their moods. When my husband gets down about something so do I, and the thing that causes him - and therefore me - huge distress is the lack of any sort of help to address the offending behaviour.

In the 7 months he was at the first prison he had four visits from the OMU (Offender Management Unit). Each visit was less than 5 minutes. It was a different person almost every time and they contradicted each other.

In the 5 months, he has been at his second prison, he has had 2 visits. Each less than 5 minutes. They have been through the cell door, in the easy hearing of anyone on the corridor.

My husband has worked hard to understand his life and what caused the offences to occur and has made progress. However, it seems that nobody in authority is aware or interested.

It is interesting and deeply disturbing that the prisoners turn to each other to try to help and sort out what has caused their offences. This isn't good enough; I believe we, as a society, are failing them.

I don't need to tell you that there is a shocking amount of suicide in prison and the thing that so often causes the deepest grief is the knowledge that their family is suffering as much, if not more than they are themselves. The families - including young children - serve the same sentence, just in a different way.

"I hate prisons in this country and everything they stand for and yet I get so much from these visits. I love standing with that amazing, eclectic group of people at the prison gates beneath the razor wire - only we know what it feels like to have this unique set of heart-breaking challenges. When someone goes to prison you damage the bonds that exist between everyone who loves and needs them; something dies. But the love and loyalty and sheer strength of character I have seen in those waiting rooms have restored my faith in humanity. I am ashamed of my former ignorance."

It would appear I am not at all unusual in standing by my husband. There is love by the bucket load in those waiting rooms. And there are no barriers; we are all there for the same reason. There are the well to do, travellers, crack addicts and everything in between. And I am in debt to every single one of them for showing me just how vast compassion can be.

One lady drives 5 hours from Sussex - a ten-hour round trip and she sets off at 5.30 in the morning. A wonderful gypsy lady covered in life's scars and ink tattoos told me she was visiting her husband and her son - both in the same prison. I said how on earth do you cope? She said you just have to keep loving them. I will never forget her.

On my first day visiting, I was so nervous I couldn't even get my key in the locker and a woman in her mid-20s, with scars where she had cut herself and needle marks all up her arms, and an aroma about her that implied she hadn't washed possibly ever, came up to me, put an arm around me and said "It's your first time, isn't it? I'll look after you." Angels come in many, many disguises.

So, you see, it is not all negative. Astonishing things have come out of the indescribable pain.

Maybe this is what a crisis can do. A crisis is a point at which change must come, for better or worse. 'Krinein' is the Greek root of the word and means to separate or sift. Crises shake things up and we emerge from them with what matters.

The crisis in my life has opened my eyes.

So although I have hurt more than I ever thought I could hurt without dying, although I have been punished by a system that doesn't seem to care about the collateral damage when someone is sent to prison for this type of offence. Still, I have lost financial security, friends and family and possibly will lose the home I love, I have gained something extraordinary and priceless.

I have gained knowledge and it is this: Kindness matters. Listening matters. Real friends stick by you no matter what. We all belong to each other - yes even, and possibly especially, the so-called dustbin people of society; they may just have the most of all to teach us. We can do hard things."

LOVE WINS!

Emma is an Administrator on a unique Facebook page, founded by former prison officer Joe Chapman called "Victims Unseen" and Rosie was one of the first to join. It is a secret Facebook group for partners, family, and friends of Sex Offenders so that they can receive advice, support and friendship from people who have suffered in the same way.

They are using their knowledge and experience to support people, which is what Joe has been doing since February 1979.

For further information on obtaining support from "Victims Unseen" please **visit www.joechapman.co.uk**

Support in Prison

Support in prison can come in many forms and from lots of different agencies but the chances are, it won't seek you out, you will have to ask for it.

One of the biggest pitfalls inside is the fact people continue the behaviour that landed them in prison in the first place. Drug users still use, alcoholics still drink, drug dealers still deal and thieves still steal.

If you carry on doing the stuff, you will carry on getting the same outcome. Nothing changes if nothing changes!

Prison should be the wake-up call you need to address the things that have gone wrong in your life and whilst we accept that that is easy for us to say, the reality is plenty of people never return to prison once they leave.

The people that never return are normally the ones that change something about themselves, perhaps they get clean, perhaps they re-establish family ties or perhaps they gain a qualification that leads to a stable job.

Change is possible, it just isn't easy.

Healthcare

We list healthcare as an excuse to get out of your cell and whilst that is true, it is a good idea to use it to make sure everything is ok.

Understand that this isn't BUPA or some fancy West London medical practice that is going to cure your baldness and give you a facelift but you can make sure that your head isn't imminently about to drop off.

You can address any minor health problems and if necessary be referred to a specialist for more serious stuff, this won't happen at the same pace as it would on the outside but it can happen.

As we already touched on, prison healthcare has been largely privatised now and they medicate for the sake of medicating which isn't always a good thing.

For example, drug replacement drugs. The idea you would give an alcoholic a small "hit" of alcohol throughout the day is absurd because all you are doing is feeding the addiction.

Abstinence based drug treatment is far more effective, perhaps not the initial withdrawal phase but long term the effects are much better, our advice would be to go down this route and avoid drug replacement treatment.

Listeners

From time to time prison might feel like too much for you, there is no shame in feeling this way because it is a lot to take in and deal with.

Sometimes the problem is as simple as just needing to offload onto someone, to talk about it. This is where listeners can help.

If you do find that it goes beyond talking, seek medical advice in the prison.

Your first port of call though will be a listener. You can request to speak to a listener at any time night or day, they work on a rota so are available at night, since nights are the hardest time in prison there may be a wait for one to get to you.

The scheme is run by the Samaritans, they train prisoners in becoming a listener using a similar framework to their call handlers but adapted for the prison environment.

So, listeners are just prisoners, this often means it is easier for people to open up to them because they know just what you are going through.

You will meet the listener in private and what you discuss is completely confidential, the same as it would be if you called their helpline on the outside.

As with life on the outside, listeners have to pass on information if there is a genuine concern or threat of serious harm to you or someone else.

Listeners aren't paid and they receive no benefit from doing this role.

You may never need to use the service but it is important to know it is there. You may even wish to volunteer to become a listener, the training is something that will serve you well post-release and a rewarding role to put yourself forward for in prison.

To find out more about the service you can visit their website: www.samaritans.org/how-we-can-help/prisons/listener-scheme/

Reps - violence reduction

Prisons are plagued by violence, we would love to be able to say they aren't but the harsh reality is that violence is a daily occurrence and it is on the rise.

Violence in prison is often the first response by people who do not know how to communicate their frustration correctly.

Year on year figures show that assaults increase by around 5% each year and self-harm, of which some can be linked to the threat of violence or witnessing the actual violence is up by around 22%.

Another contributing factor to violence is the spiralling mental health crisis that has swept through UK prisons.

To combat this and in an indirect way an admission that the cuts to staff have had an impact; prisons have launched violence reduction reps.

Like most reps and orderlies these are prisoners just like you.

The violence reduction reps however are slightly different, they tend to be prisoners that carry a certain level of respect and someone that the wing might look up to.

There is a reason for this if someone you respect has come to your door to request you stop bullying someone you are more likely to pay attention to than if an officer asked.

Their role should be to try and mediate on wings and reduce violence through talking.

Their title may vary from prison to prison but they will exist in some capacity in every single UK jail.

Whilst some of the reps will do what the job entails some view this role as an opportunity, they use the information gained for their benefit.

This is a problem of having prisoners run certain elements of the prison procedures, the responsibilities of some of the roles can be exploited for personal gain, this is especially true in the role of violence reduction reps.

By recruiting people with a certain respect level there is every chance they are involved in the problems they are supposed to help resolve.

We suggest you air on the side of caution when talking to them, serious problems and concerns should be raised with your personal officer.

Prison discipline system

Prisons are run by the Governors but they have set guidelines and rules that they all follow. These are referred to as PSI's (prison service instructions) and PSO's (prison service orders).

These as you would perhaps expect are lengthy and at times difficult to understand - there are books on the market that are costly, bulky and extremely wordy but they break down each rule and regulation if you require.

To give you an idea the PSI for prison discipline is 87 pages long. You will see them around the prison and they will look like this:

A full list of prison rules, PSI's and PSO's can be found online at www.justice.gov.uk/offenders.

HM Prison & Probation Service

PRISONER DISCIPLINE PROCEDURES (ADJUDICATIONS)	
This instruction applies to: -	Reference: -
Prisons	PSI 05/2018
Issue Date	**Effective Date**
21/12/2018	01/02/2019
Issued on the authority of	HMPPS Agency Board
For action by (Who is this instruction for)	All staff responsible for the development and publication of policy and instructions *(Double click in box, as appropriate)* ☐ HMPPS HQ ☒ Public Sector Prisons ☒ Contracted Prisons* ☐ National Probation Service (NPS) ☐ Community Rehabilitation Companies (CRCs) ☒ HMPPS Immigration Removal Centres (IRCs) ☐ Other Providers of Probation and Community Services ☒ Governors ☐ Heads of Groups ** If this box is marked, then in this document the term Governor also applies to Directors of Contracted Prisons*
Instruction type	Service Specification for Prisoner Discipline and Segregation Legal compliance
For information	All staff in prisons who have contact with prisoners, staff in HMPPS headquarters who deal with adjudication appeals
Provide a summary of the policy aim and the reason for its development / revision	This instruction replaces and consolidates PSI 47/2011 Prisoner Discipline Procedures and PSI 31/2013 Recovery of Monies for Damage to Prisons and Prison Property. It provides essential policy updates to support front line staff in undertaking effective adjudications. This is an interim PSI ahead of a forthcoming Policy Framework following a wider review of the current system of disciplining prisoners to support Prison Reform. The adjudication paperwork and training for adjudicators and staff will also be refreshed and updated.
Contact	Deregulation and Operational Policy Team, Justice Analysis and Offender Policy Group, Ministry of Justice Operational_policy1@justice.gov.uk
Associated documents	PSO 1700 Segregation and Reviewing and Authorising: Continuing Segregation and Temporary Confinement in Special Accommodation (2015) PSO 3601 Mandatory Drug Testing PSO 4600 Unconvicted, Unsentenced and Civil Prisoners PSO 4800 Women Prisoners PSI 31/2009 Compact Based Drug Testing

In addition to the standard universal rules, individual prisons may have additional rules and guidelines they implement.

We have provided a summary of the standard discipline procedure below:

Breaking the rules is referred to as an offence, you can be charged for an offence and subsequently punished.

The punishment will be appropriate to the offence and in the most severe of cases referred to the police or visiting judge.

A summary of the rules you may have broken are:

- Behaving in a way that could offend, threaten or hurt someone else.
- Stopping prison staff from doing their jobs
- Escaping from prison (or attempting/planning to escape)
- Drugs and alcohol
- Causing damage to the prison
- Having something that you should not or cannot have or having more of something than you should have (knife, property, mobile phone etc.)
- Being in a place in the prison that you shouldn't be
- Not doing what prison staff tell you to do
- Breaking the rules whilst you are out of prison (temporary release on license, hospital visit, community work etc.)

Complaints procedure

In prison, as in life, you may feel that something has happened to you that is unfair or unjust that leads to you either missing out or being hard done by in some way.

This is part and parcel of everyday life, most of the time it can be resolved amicably by speaking about it.

However, if after speaking to the person involved or your personal officer you still feel the problem is either not solved, not solved adequately or you feel someone simply hasn't done their job you can still complain and take things further.

The first place to start is the good old app system, complaint apps should be readily available on the wing and there should be no need to request one from an officer - this begins the internal complaints procedure. This will need to be done within 3 months of the incident you wish to complain about.

Once you have filled out your complaint app, remember to keep a copy, you will return it to the wing office where there should be a box specific for complaints.

The only difference to the procedure I just mentioned is if your complaint is about being discriminated against, these forms are requested from the wing office and are often called DIRF forms (Discrimination Incident Report Form).

The theory is complaints are confidential but this rouse is soon uncovered when you find out that the prison staff are the ones that investigate the complaint themselves.

Once you have received your response it is then up to you to decide if you wish to take it further because you don't feel the outcome is satisfactory.

If that is the case you will then need to contact the IMB (Independent Monitoring Board).

The IMB can be contacted at any time but they are more likely to "investigate" a complaint if the correct prison complaints procedure has been followed in the first place.

The IMB are a group of people that are hired by the Government to act as the watchdog for prisons.

In our experience because they are hired by the Government they tend not to rock the boat, so what they say in person is likely to be understanding and encouraging but the reality is they very rarely go against the status quo.

If you are still unhappy then you have two choices either instruct a legal team to argue your case, in the case of injury or some form of damage claim you will find plenty of "no win, no fee" firms in the inside times.

Or you can complain to the Prisons and Probation Ombudsman - it won't surprise you to learn that this process is not quick, it can take months for a reply but since time is something prisoners tend to have a lot of, you shouldn't be in short supply of it.

Complaints are often passed up to the main Governor, again from experience this is never much more than lip service to give the illusion that it is being taken seriously.

Progressing with your sentence

Alternative therapies

Before his last sentence, Terry was introduced to a book called "we're all doing time" by Bo Lozoff, where an introduction to yoga and its benefits was discussed.

Terry used these techniques throughout his sentence and credits it, in part, to his willingness to seek out therapy at HMP Grendon.

Terry went on to write about his time in Grendon and how elements of it have had a positive impact on him turning his around.

Terry and I use the same holistic health and wellness coach, Colette from Nourish Wellness Sanctuary.

Whilst she hasn't managed to successfully dissuade either of us from cake and biscuits, which is actually the point - it isn't about do's and don'ts it is about knowing you have the power to choose, she has managed to help us to make more thoughtful choices in life and build on the therapy that Terry experienced in HMP Grendon (Grendon's Therapy - The Inside Story by Terry Ellis. Available on Amazon).

We asked her to write the next section of the book for us to introduce to you, some of the skills, techniques and strategies to becoming a more rounded and accepting person.

Colette isn't a former inmate nor does she work inside the prison environment, however, her teachings can and should be adapted to help cope inside prison.

We asked Colette to give us a brief foreword to her section about mindfulness and general well-being.

"I would like people to notice how much of their attention is in the past or the future. Don't judge or analyse it, just observe the reaction, watch the thought and feel the emotion.

Identification with and attachment to the thought or emotion is what gives it more energy and momentum. Just watch it and let it go. Imagine yourself standing on the earth, feeling grounded, as you watch your thoughts drift by like clouds.

Acceptance of what is, without resistance and blame, brings the power to choose and change."

"Accept - the act. Whatever the present moment contains, accept it as if you had chosen it. Always work with it, not against it."
- Eckhart Tolle -

This resonates with Terry because a large section of the therapy he writes about in Grendon's Therapy - The Inside Story, is about accepting what we cannot change and living in the moment.

Mindfulness

Adjusting to change can be difficult, we need to accept that what is happening on the outside of us does not define who we are on the inside. We are in charge of our own internal mood and can use tools to promote health and well-being even in difficult circumstances. One of these tools is meditation, simply put, awareness.

This is especially true in prison, you will be tested daily by external factors, whether it is the prison officer telling you to fill out another app, the inmate that cuts in line whilst queuing for dinner or the cellmate snoring - knowing that you are in control of how you react will be integral to you getting through your sentence as trouble-free as possible.

Meditation and mindfulness are terms that conjure up images of people sitting cross-legged, chanting and often associated with monks. However, the reality is that mindfulness can be as simple as just stopping to take a few deep breaths.

Those few moments are all it takes to bring focus and attention back to present moment awareness, snapping out of auto-pilot and habitual thinking.

This again is especially true in prison because you are monitored 24/7 and the way you might act on the outside could land you in a whole heap of trouble on the inside. Taking a moment, by taking a deep breath will give you the time and space required to evaluate the situation and consider whether or not your normal reaction is worth it.

This doesn't mean aiming to live this way in every moment, we are human after all with a predisposition to get caught up in past and future thinking. Think of taking a deep breath as a bit like pressing the pause button, living in the now, one conscious breath at a time.

It creates space in your mind to step back from the pull of external factors, the constant overstimulation from the other prisoners, the officers, the noises, the other arguments and the regular prison banter.

That space can bring the opportunity for a fresh perspective, more focus and a sense of calm. It is detaching from everything outside that is grasping for attention all of the time and instead of rediscovering the power in choosing and responding rather than reacting.

**"Now is the only true reality.
Be Here. Live It. Breathe It In."**

There are many forms of meditation practices and ways to bring mindfulness to everyday life.

Let's start with the breath.

You can do this wherever you are, at any time. Standing, sitting, lying in bed, on the bus, in the supermarket, in the dinner queue, during movement or in the exercise yard.

Just take three, slow, deep breaths - in through the nose and out through the mouth.

As you breathe in, feel your chest rise and stomach/diaphragm expand - you can place your hand on your stomach at the base of your rib cage if you like.

As you breathe out, feel the release - you can drop your shoulders and let out a sigh.

It's as simple as that.

And yet the breath is a powerful tool to not only create a mindful moment but can be used to energise or relax the body and mind.

Have you ever seen a footballer step up to take an important penalty? They all take a few deep breaths before they start their run-up.

There are variations and ways to build upon this mindful breathing exercise. Approach them with a sense of curiosity and willingness to try something new.

Variations:

Counting in your mind '1' as you breathe in and '2' as you breathe out.

When you reach '10', start from '1' again.

You will notice that you'll likely lose track of your count, either reaching upwards of 10 before realising or forgetting to count at all as you drift off into your thoughts.

The aim here is just to notice when this happens and return to the breath (starting at '1') as many times as necessary. It is building concentration and resilience.

<u>Mantras/Affirmations</u> can shift your attention and energy to be more positive and uplifting, with an intention that feels good to you.

Prison is a time that will test your resolve, as has been discussed at length in this book, mental health issues are rife in prison and this technique is an excellent way to transcend your surroundings.

Ask yourself, what feelings do you desire to cultivate? Choose words and phrases that are life-affirming, your preferred states of being. Do you want to feel grounded and calm? Energised and inspired? Grateful and warm-hearted? Try saying the following phrases in your mind as you breathe and use the <u>one</u> that resonates with you, or choose your own.

Breathe in: *I am*
Breathe out: *Calm*

Breathe in: *I feel*
Breathe out: *Vibrant*

Breathe in: *I release all judgement/negativity*
Breathe out: *<release breath and imagine letting it go>*

Breathe in: *I walk through life powerfully present/confident*
Breathe out: *<release the breath and imagine embodying this energy>*

You can continue this for as long as you like, being sure to keep the focus on the breath, but just a few rounds are enough to break the cycle and bring awareness back to reality.

"If my environment dictates my mood, then my life will feel like a roller coaster. The way to steady ground is through my breath"
- Gabrielle Bernstein -

A little hack on the outside is to set a phone alert throughout the day as a reminder to take a breath, in prison you could choose the door to unlock, association and daily movement schedule as your reminder cue.

In time, taking some slow deep, mindful breaths through the day will become natural and those breaths can become a new response in times of discomfort, stress or situations which trigger a strong emotional charge.

Use mindfulness to tune into what feels good and that suits your current state of being, for example, when restless in the body or mind, it can be helpful to try a movement-based mindful activity to release some of the energy, to enable a more settled and grounded meditation practice. The aim remains to be conscious and aware of the present moment and experience.

<u>Loving Kindness Meditation</u>

This meditation is about setting a loving intention, without expectation of anything in return. Said out loud, or in our mind, we focus on cultivating care and friendly feelings, first for ourselves.

When you feel ready, gently extend your warm wishes by repeating the phrases while imagining and directing them towards others - a loved one, friend or acquaintance.

This technique is one that can be applied before making a phone call home, it is very easy to be negative about prison and the surroundings you find yourself in, phone calls should be the time to escape from the prison (not literally). Having positive phone calls will help you have a positive day/night.

When you feel ready, expand your offering to include those who ignite negativity within you. Adjust the intention to match that which connects with and inspires you.

May I be happy
May I be healthy
May I be safe
May I be at peace

May you be happy
May you be healthy
May you be safe
May you be at peace

May we all be happy
May we all be healthy
May we all be safe
May we all be at peace

"The rule in loving kindness practice is to follow the way that most easily opens your heart"
- Jack Kornfield -

Mindful Movement

Mindful movement creates balance and unites the mind and body. It brings awareness to bodily sensations which act as messengers and are a cue to take action upon noticing pain or discomfort, which could otherwise go unnoticed until it becomes more severe.

Movement also helps to release stress and restless energy, especially when experiencing strong emotions and can even remedy sleepiness. Often, we try to think our way out of a feeling or we wait for an external circumstance to ignite a shift within. A quick, simple and effective way to change your state, is to move.

Applied to a prison environment, it is extremely easy to lie on your bed getting wound up by the noises your cellmate is making, you can lie there and allow the annoyance to grow or you can break the focus by getting up and moving around.

Movement can consist of stretching, yoga, a cell workout, dance etc.

Never push beyond your natural limits with mindful movement exercises. The aim is to release tension rather than exert force.

<u>Stretching:</u>

Gently stretching the muscles releases pockets of tension that would otherwise prevent us from achieving the relaxation we seek. This can also be achieved with a technique in meditation called muscle relaxation, whereby each area of the body is tensed and then released.

You can also perform any stretches you are already familiar with, but incorporate mindfulness by observing and bringing awareness to the bodily sensations before, during and after the stretch. Be slow, gentle and hold each stretch for at least a few breaths.

Stretches can be particularly beneficial upon waking to ease stiffness, counteract stagnant energy and stimulate blood flow.

I have been informed that prison beds are not the most comfortable so it is not uncommon to wake each day with various aches, pains and stiffness - so a daily stretch when you wake is highly recommended.

Dance:

This is something that you may wish to do when your cellmate has left the cell but certainly shouldn't be discounted simply because of where you are.

Play a song, anything you want and "dance like no one is watching!" It might feel silly or awkward at first, but release those judgements and labels of "good and bad". Shake out the anxiety, anger, frustration, the feeling of being stuck or lazy and just have fun with it!

Notice how it feels to move in different ways.

Take a few moments of stillness (sit or lie down) after any of these exercises to let your body and mind integrate and absorb the benefits.

Yoga

Simple yoga routines are something that are becoming increasingly popular inside UK prisons and follows on perfectly from mindful movement.

Yoga is a great way to start the day as it helps stretch out the muscles and wakes you up.

As with any form of movement/exercise, we advise that you consult a doctor if you have health concerns and stop immediately if you feel any discomfort or pain.

What we will introduce you to is a very basic routine that helps with mindful breathing and movement.

The Sun Salutation is 12 linked movements with the original idea being that you show gratitude to the sun and can be traced back as far as the 9th Century where it is believed to have started in India.

History lesson aside, the following graphic shows the 12 movements/poses.

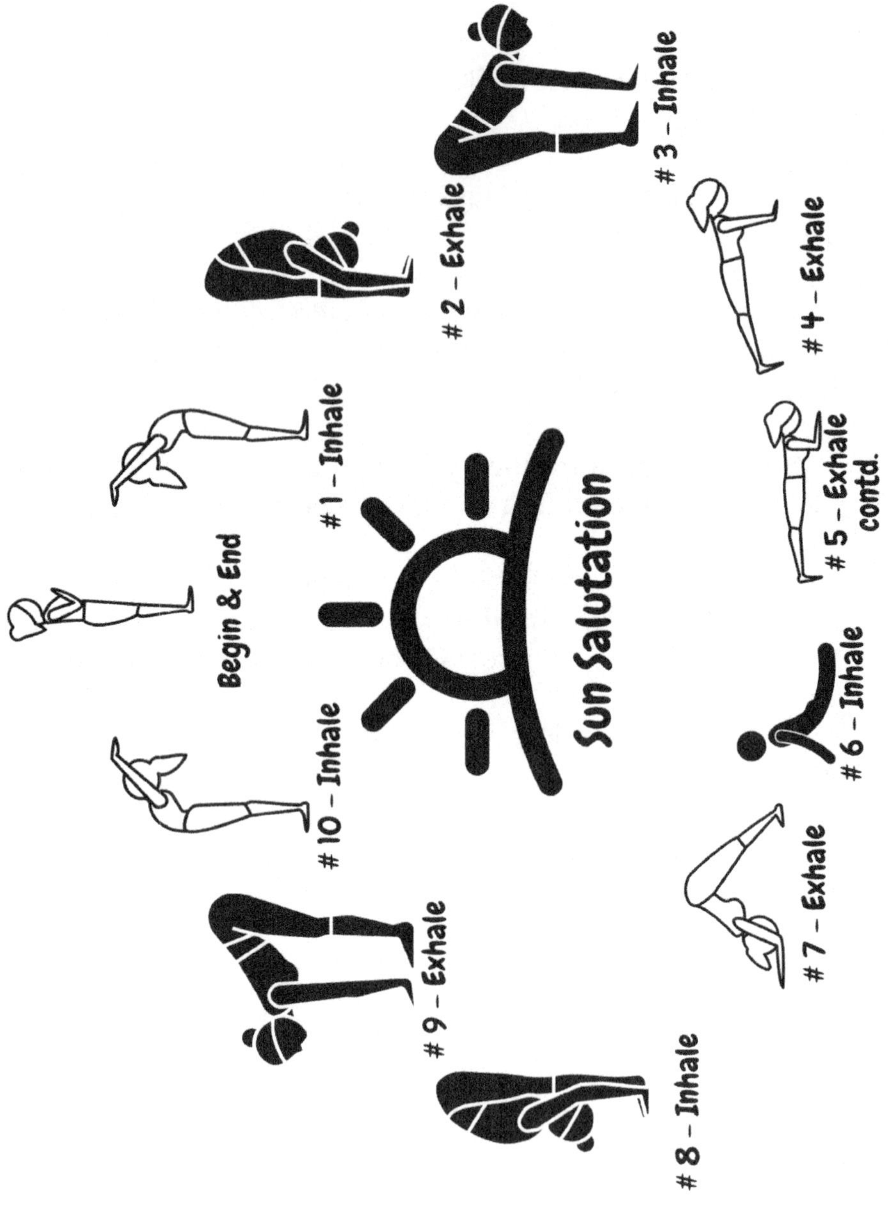
Sun Salutation
Begin & End
1 – Inhale
2 – Exhale
3 – Inhale
4 – Exhale
5 – Exhale contd.
6 – Inhale
7 – Exhale
8 – Inhale
9 – Exhale
10 – Inhale

Begin and End - Stand tall, feet firmly on the ground with your hands together on your chest.
1. **Inhale -** Lift your hands (keeping them together, as if praying) over your head, lean your hips forward and arch your back - whilst performing take a deep breath in.
2. **Exhale -** Lean your chest forward, knees slightly bent and fold inwards. During the movement, you should exhale.
3. **Inhale -** Lift your head and rise back up about halfway so your back is flat. During the movement start to take in a deep breath.
4. **Exhale -** Move both feet back, keep your arms straight with your shoulders over your wrists, so that you transition into the plank position - start to exhale.
5. **Exhale continued -** as you continue to exhale lower your chest, knees and chin towards the floor, keeping your elbows tucked in.
6. **Inhale -** Now as you breathe in straighten your legs and feet, arch your back backwards and raise your head and chest.
7. **Exhale -** Lift your bum/tailbone, push back onto your feet, keep your back straight and your knees slightly bent. Breathe out.
8. **Inhale -** Bring your feet forward between your hands, keep your knees slightly bent and fold inwards. Take a deep breath in.
9. **Exhale -** Come back up about halfway, keeping your back flat and exhale.
10. **Inhale -** Raise, extend your arms over your head, arch your back slightly and take a deep breath in before exhaling and returning to your starting position.

Congratulations, you have just completed your first yoga routine.

Things like yoga are easily discarded in prison as mumbo jumbo but they have incredible benefits and genuinely help you stay in a positive frame of mind.

We recommend that whilst doing anything like this, focus on what you are grateful for and what makes you happy, forget for the time being you are performing it in prison and transcend the walls of the prison to a better place.

Health and Nutrition

Prison menus are limited at best so it may seem strange that we have a section on Health and Nutrition but just because your choices are limited it doesn't mean that you can't make more mindful selections.

Typically, you will get a piece of fruit every day as part of one of your meal packs, fresh fruit and veg are at a premium in prison so take the opportunity to eat them. You could also save up your oranges and make yourself orange juice once a week or chop up the fruit and have it in your porridge or cereal each day.

During your meal selections, you can also be mindful of the selections you make, for example, a jacket potato and beans is the better option over a sausage roll.

Generally, the vegetarian options are slightly bigger than the meat options so you get a little more when selecting the healthier choice but you will struggle to eat healthily every day, it is very much the case that you just have to be mindful of your selections.

If you are concerned about your weight you can speak to healthcare, most prisons will offer some form of dietary assistance through their healthcare provider and they will be able to give you food diaries and guidance on what you eat.

Nutrition is a significant foundational part of wellness. Healthy eating is crucial if you want to feel and look the best you possibly can.

Nourishment is more than just food, it's whole body wellness and comprises of stress management which can be achieved through mindfulness, meditation, nature, rest, hydration, relaxation and connection.

We have obtained an example of the weekly menu choice inside a prison - the picture isn't fantastic but it is a good example of what is on offer:

Return menu to the post boxes located in **Dining Hall by 18.00HRS SUNDAY**
(If you do not return your menu, you will be given option 1 for lunch & 7 for dinner only)
* Items marked with this symbol contains ingredient produced from genetically modified Maize or Soya.

Halal
Vegetarian
Healthy Eat
Vegan

THURSDAY

LUNCH			DINNER		
Cheese Melt	) (	①	Halal Chicken and Mushroom Pie		) (
Ham & Pickle	☺	2	Cheese & Onion Quiche	⊛	) (
(V)Falafel & Sweet/Sour - VEGAN	☺ ⊛) (✧	3	Spicy Chicken Pasty	⊛	) (
Vegetable Soup with 1/2 Baguette	☺ ⊛) (✧	4	Lentil & Mushroom Bake	☺ ⊛	) (

FRIDAY

LUNCH			DINNER		
Cheese Melt	⊛) (	1	Battered Cod		) (
Cajun Tuna and Peppers	) (	②	Cajun Burger & Roll		
Ham & Onion	☺	3	Vegetable Burger	☺ ⊛	) (
Sausage Chopped & pickle (V)	☺ ⊛) (✧	4	Cheese & Onion Pasty	☺ ⊛	) (

SATURDAY

LUNCH			DINNER		
Cheese Melt	⊛) (	1	Halal Chicken Leg Tandoori		
Chicken Mayonnaise (H)	) (	2	Fish Fillet in a Mushroom Sauce	⊛	
Sausage Roll (Hot)	) (	③	Vegetable Pancake Roll	⊛	
Vegetable Pasty	☺ ⊛) (✧	4	(V) Stirfry Vegetable & Fried Rice	⊛	

SUNDAY

LUNCH			DINNER		
Halal Roast Chicken & Stuffing	) (	①	Cheese Melt		⊛
Roast Gammon & Apple sauce		2	Vegetable Pasty	☺ ⊛	
(V) Broccoli Pasta Bake	☺ ⊛) (✧	3	Beef & Onion	☺	
Vegetable Samosa	⊛) (✧	4	(V)Falafel & Sweet/Sour - VEGAN	☺ ⊛	

MONDAY

LUNCH			DINNER		
Cheese Melt	⊛) (	1	Halal Beef Bolognaise		
Tuna & Cucumber	) (	②	Tuna Pasta Salad	☺	
Ham & Mustard	⊛	3	Cous Cous Filled Pepper	☺	
Vegetable Soup with 1/2 Baguette	☺ ⊛) (✧	4	Vegetable Kiev x1	☺	

TUESDAY

LUNCH			DINNER		
Cheese Melt	⊛) (	1	Fish Fingers x5		
Beef & Onion	☺) (	2	Beef Steaklette x2 & Fried Onions		
Ham & Tomato	☺	3	Vegetable Burger	⊛	
Baked Potato & Veg Curry	☺ ⊛) (✧	④	Lasagne Pie		

WEDNESDAY

LUNCH			DINNER		
Cheese Melt	⊛) (	①	Halal Turkey Korma		
Sliced Turkey & Mayo		2	Savory Minced Beef		
Ham & Onion	☺	3	Spinach & Lentil Curry		
		4	Tuna Pasta Salad		

Final Thought

Energy is always being directed into something - stress, procrastination, rumination, soul-nourishing, life-affirming thoughts and actions.

Choose to bring in more light and mindfulness into each day. Ask yourself: Does this (thought/action/experience) feel heavy or light?

Bring balance by connecting the mind with the body through the breath, movement or meditation. Embrace each moment with a sense of wonder, gratitude and joy.

This will really resonate with you when you leave prison, in those first few days out, you will suddenly appreciate the small things that you had previously taken for granted - the birds singing, the local nature, your bed, your pet dog - the list is endless but you will notice things much more.

> **"Growth is what happens when we walk the path of mindfulness"**
> **- Lena Franklin -**

Drug and Alcohol programs

We firmly believe that you should go into prison with an open mind and that you should have the sole aim of leaving prison a better person than the one that went in.

At no point have we sugar-coated prison, self-improvement will be a challenge because it is easy to coast through a sentence doing what you did on the outside and being bitter at the system that took away your freedom.

Your offence may have had nothing to do with drink or drugs but that doesn't mean they were not a problem.

There is a preconception of a drug addict that often has frail, drug-addled bodies strewn across squats in disused and abandoned buildings with little to no cognitive function left.

However, addiction covers a broad spectrum of things and prison is the perfect time to address these.

So, even if you truly believe you don't have a problem it is worth speaking to the drug and alcohol teams because you might not have a better time to access them.

I had a problem with cocaine, this wasn't so much a physical addiction because I could genuinely stop at any time.

That was what I used to do convince myself that it wasn't an addiction - I would stop taking it for a week, a month, at one stage I stopped taking it for six months and that was the confirmation I needed that I didn't have a problem.

I eventually faced up to the fact I did have a problem, I had a good job, earned good money and enjoyed a decent life but I used cocaine to escape facets of my life where I was deeply unhappy.

What I learned very quickly was that I was not alone as an addict and that there were very specific triggers to my drug use - the same as every other addict.

Some gamble, some drink, some take coke and others use heroin - there is no difference to any of them and there is no shame in standing up and admitting that you are an addict.

Drug and alcohol teams provide a service that, in our own experiences go far beyond just recovery, they offer an outlet in a difficult environment to talk.

Talking about things that you have bottled and helping you understand the reason you have taken the paths in your life that you have.

As you will by now have noticed, Terry is a very vocal advocate for talking therapies and he became a peer mentor on the drug-free wing in HMP Springhill where he helped people talk about their problems and maintain a drug-free lifestyle.

Terry is drug and alcohol-free for 8 years, 4 of which have been since release from prison.

I am 6 years drug-free and whilst I haven't been a big drinker in those 6 years I did use to have the occasional drink, 2 years I ago I stopped that as well.

Utilising the support networks available to you, when they are available to you can help, step one is recognising that you have a problem at all and the biggest hurdle for many people to overcome.

The prison whether or not you say you have a problem and whether or not your offence was drink or drug-related will expect you to have your initial meeting with the drug and alcohol teams, failure to do so will be a "black" against your name.

This will be taken into consideration on your prison record when they assess you for TAG (early release on an electronic monitoring bracelet) or for probation.

Vulnerable Prisoners - This is your life - The OASYS

Usually, just after the anniversary of your Sentencing date, you will be presented with a document called an OASYS, which stands for "Offender Assessment SYStem". The Prison Service has gone to great expense to employ an army of psychologists who will welcome you as their new specimen. Remember Sex-Offenders are big business!

Like it or not, your life is in the hands of professionals and they will decide how risky you are, often without speaking to you at all, or checking the accuracy of the information that was used to convict you. The information is mainly gathered from CPS records, so no defence info is used.

Once convicted, you are guilty as charged and must accept that you will be held wherever the Prison Service sees fit, anywhere within the UK, and you will probably find yourself sharing a cell.

Even if you feel the verdict was wrong, (which most may claim in the early stages) it's not a good start to introduce yourself as innocent, and therefore not happy to be in the company of "nonces". You are going to need all the friends you can find as you settle in, and you will soon discover that you are in good company on the VP wing, as most people have a big investment in staying safe and looking out for each other.

Believe it or not, there is even a hierarchy amongst sex offenders, so you must not be tempted to reveal every detail of your crimes to the first person who winks at you, or to minimise your guilt to try to stay at the bottom of the league table. You may find yourself indulging in a little trip down "Felony Lane" with others, but remember to keep anything you hear to yourself, repeating information you have gathered within earshot of other prisoners or "screws" can get you into deep water.

It's also worth remembering that you are under constant scrutiny, and the list of "Risk Factors" that you own will follow you through your sentence and beyond. Depending on your offences, your approach to female officers (or male), communication with civilian workers and visitors, relationships with other prisoners, what you watch on TV, what you like reading and who you communicate with outside or have visits from, are recorded for future reference.

At some point, you should be given an "Induction" which will provide all of the information you need to survive within the confines of the VP wing.

Although there is a line drawn between "screws and cons" the boundaries are often blurred, but you will soon work out who the friendly officer is, and who the ones are to give a wide birth to.

COURSEWORK

The more intensive Sex Offender Programmes, such as Kaizen, should be targeted at high and medium risk offenders. There is good evidence that indiscriminate allocation to any programmes is ineffective and may be counterproductive. The belief is that that you will only benefit from interventions that are meaningful to you and are delivered in a way that is appropriate to your learning style. Also, the needs of particular groups (e.g. women, ethnic minorities, those with learning difficulties) must be considered. Interventions should be paced, and you should be granted the opportunity to practise new skills/attitudes and behaviour.

Hopefully, you will be motivated to take part in the various courses available. Even if you are not completely motivated to do them, or you think you know it all anyway, the courses offered are used to monitor whether you are following your "Sentence Plan", and if you are not following it you won't progress! However, if you are found unsuited to courses, you can still progress OK. There is a vast difference between being unsuited, opposed to being "Unready"

Beware of anybody who says it's not worth it. They are not serving your sentence ... you are!

The OASYS "must provide a broad classification of the likelihood of reconviction within a given time frame. It must separately identify the serious risk of harm should further offences occur and to whom the risk of harm is posed and in what circumstances. It must provide an offending related needs profile, and direct steps to reduce these needs. It must identify the prisoner's ability and motivation to change, and any other factors that could affect the individual's response to a specific course."

In short, it is your very own crystal ball that the Offender Management Unit use to predict your future.

It is designed to:
- Determine the likelihood of you being reconvicted.
- To identify and classify your offending related needs, including problems with your personality and thought processes.
- Assess the risk of serious harm you pose to others, even to yourself.
- To help with the management of those risks
- To link everything into your Sentence Plan and supervision sessions.
- To decide if you need any further "Specialist Assessments".
- To measure your change during the period of your sentence and supervision.

The Prison Service state "The assessment system must be constructed so that the items in it make sense to the assessor and the offender. It must be clear why each item is included. Only if the value of collecting information is readily recognised can we expect practitioners to conduct the assessments conscientiously and fairly and accurately."

The reality can be very different, as you may struggle to get a copy of your assessment, It is not always made clear at all why certain items have been included, and if the document is false, misleading or inaccurate it is difficult but not impossible to change it!

MAKING A COMPLAINT:

Your Offender Manager who agrees to the content can be ultimately taken to court for any false information. It is the Outside Probation Officer who must be given the opportunity to resolve the situation but be courteous and polite in your communication. Remember, it must be the facts you are disputing, not their opinion unless the opinion is presented as fact.

The content can be changed under the PSI instructions which govern the control and use of the assessment.

If the Probation Offender Manager refuses to change it you must then take your complaint to Probation Service ACO, and always keep a copy of the documents you send, and the replies you receive. If it is not supported at this level, you should then send a complaint to the Information Commissioner's Office.

Before taking it to court you must give verbal notice to the OM that you will be taking them to court, followed up in 14 days by written notice, called a "Letter Before Action." This letter should be sent by recorded delivery and followed up by a call a couple of weeks later stating that you intend to take them to court under The Data Protection Act, specifically "Informing a Data Controller of the holding of inaccurate data, with refusal to rectify."

If it goes to court you can attend, or ask a legal rep to assist, you can produce reliable evidence that you attempted to resolve it without court action. The judges respect this, and often apologise on behalf of the Probation Service and order them to make changes.

The Data Protection Act is an act of parliament and it is a criminal offence to break it; OMs have been convicted in the past, albeit given suspended sentences. You should find the new OM who is assigned, is more than willing to open up a dialogue about changing it.

They also state "It is important that offenders can express their views. MANY probation officers welcome the opportunity for offenders to complete a questionnaire about their problems. This is included in OASys as the 'Self-assessment'."

This should be the case for all prisoners, but it rarely is ... Get a copy of your OASYS and go through it, making sure that you list everything you feel is wrong.

There are 5 main parts to an OASYS, which are:

1. The risk of reconviction and offending related factors (OASys 1 and 2)
2. The risk of serious harm risks to individual and other risks
3. The OASys summary sheet
4. The Supervision and Sentence Planning
5. The Self-Assessment.

ALL OF THIS is important for you and your loved ones to know, and to keep a check on as you move through your sentence.

Also note .... There is also a 'Confidential' section for information that cannot be disclosed to you, and a form for requesting information from anyone contributing to your OASys assessment.

ANY FALSE, MISLEADING OR INACCURATE INFORMATION WILL BE USED TO ASSESS YOU IN CUSTODY, ON RELEASE AND FOR THE REMAINDER OF

YOUR TIME ON A Sexual Harm Prevention Order and or the Sexual Offenders Register

Vulnerable Prisoners - The Kaizen Course

The latest response to treating Sexual Offenders is a programme called Kaizen, which is a Japanese word meaning "Change". It replaced the discredited Sex Offenders Treatment Programme (SOTP).

For many prisoners, a better word for this course might be "Kamikaze" as some prisoners, particularly those on IPP sentences (Indeterminate Sentences for Public Protection, with no release date) have been left feeling suicidal, having realised that the findings at the end of this programme have recommended further work, potentially adding years to their time in jail.

It is yet another course, designed by psychologists who have a classroom mentality and believe that the "one size fits all approach" will be an effective method of dealing with the complex needs of offenders, although it claims to be flexible enough to suit each individual.

The course is supposed to concentrate on a person's strengths and be focused on building a positive future rather than dwelling on the past.

It is also supposed to address the issues of adults who are assessed as being a high or very high risk but is not suitable for low or medium risk Sexual Offenders. It is also used for men with General

Violent Offences and those convicted of Intimate Partner Violence. (Domestic Violence)

It is designed for all, and to meet the needs of the person rather than their type of offence, to include men who have difficulties doing offending behaviour work, forming therapeutic relationships, or they may be denying their crimes.

Kaizen will eventually replace the Healthy Relationships Programme (HRP), the Extended Sex Offender Treatment Programme (ESOTP) and the Self-Change Programme (SCP).

The prison service states it is "Brain-Friendly", and flexible enough for the various responses of the men taking part.

Extra Targets are added for sexual offenders, with the emphasis on self-discovery. To support men with low motivation, poor engagement, behaviour that interferes with treatment (stemming from insecure relationships, trauma, and unhelpful thoughts and actions)

The frequency of the group sessions can vary, the groups can be of varied sizes and be different in terms of how long the sessions last. It can fit around work or Education etc and allows for breaks if people are struggling for whatever reason.

The programme aims to reduce criminal attitudes and the likelihood of offending again.

IN THEORY:

In theory, it provides a more efficient and effective way to train prison staff.

Men will meet the criteria to do the programme if they are assessed as High risk using various assessments and they should be in high need of treatment.

A Kaizen Treatment Manager must decide the individual meets the definition of "high priority" by considering if he was to be living in the community tomorrow, with his current plans, he would have a significant risk of committing a violent or sexual offence, or violence against an intimate partner, which would lead to serious physical or extreme psychological harm from which the victim would find it difficult or impossible to recover.

Where a man does not meet all of these criteria, for example, if they are assessed as medium risk, a clinical override can be made, so they can do the course.

The Programme includes a "Success Wheel" which shows how the man is strengthening positive relationships, with pro-social support. (Support from partners, family and friends who understand the risks)

They are taught to manage life's problems, for those who are impulsive or have low self-control. To promote healthy thinking related to their offending and healthy sex, as opposed to unhealthy sex.

They look at grievance thinking (holding Grudges), and/or hostility towards others, being around anti-social peers, having a lack of intimacy with adults, feeling inadequate, sexual jealousy and emotional identification with children.

They may have difficulties solving life's problems because they are impulsive or unstable. This may be through substance abuse, handling emotions badly, or having attitudes that support partner violence.

There may be attitudes that support sexual offending, with hostile attitudes towards women, or beliefs that support child abuse.

Men need to be motivated towards stopping that behaviour.

They should be ready to engage with employment or other activities, as well as forming constructive professional and personal relationships, valuing rules, and wanting to be a responsible member of the community or family.

The Offence Related targets to deal with as regards Sexual Offenders concern Sexual preoccupation.

All of this is referred to as "The Bio-Psycho-Social model of change" and the programme proposes that risk factors are formed by underlying and interacting biological processes, both genetic and neurobiological factors, as well as developmental experiences and early learning, including attachments.

It looks at thoughts and personality, and any cultural or social influences. Which help to explain why an individual offends.

KEY PRINCIPALS:

That the length of the programme is long enough to cover the risk involved. The average full length, called the "dose" is 160 hours (68 group sessions and 11 individual sessions) but "Rolling Format" means it can be flexible and responds to any variations in an individual's risk and need.

Biological, psychological, and social circumstances make people vulnerable to offending and affect their ability to engage fully and respond to coursework.

They may have problems in their personal functioning, suspicion towards others and anti-authority views.

The programme aims to get over these using the pictorial Success Wheel, and Old me/New Me, modules, which I will explain later.

To engage those with "resistance to authority" it uses "Supportive Authority" and the 'Strategy of Choices' with a range of 'brain friendly' approaches to learning.

The Need Principle is divided into strengthening a person's biological (neurocognitive), psychological and social resources:

Strengthening of biological resources, such as the function of the brain and thought processes. Believing that the brain is adaptable and can create new pathways, which reflect new learning, resources, and skills.

Kaizen, therefore, includes mindfulness techniques such as 'Here and Now', self-monitoring techniques, repetition of good practices and problem-solving training, which have all been found to strengthen an individual's thought processes.

It strengthens psychological resources, such as flexibility between thoughts and emotions and gaining empathy with others. And it does this by strengthening healthy thinking, developing insight and awareness, providing knowledge to help offenders develop personal rules (New Me) and better emotional management

All this requires what they call a "therapeutic alliance" between facilitators and participants, helping the process of self-discovery and reflecting back.

Strengthening of social resources is called "social capital, which means developing an individual's skills to engage fully with communities, family etc. and creating positive relationships (citizenship). It is also about improving the number of social resources that they have to draw on for more support (social capital).

It does this by teaching participants to develop their interpersonal skills using skills practice and encouraging the development of social support networks. (Family plays a big part here)

Strengthening the intention to stop offending by helping people to develop resources which will strengthen the intention not to re-offend.

This is done by setting personal goals, motivating men to consider and try 'change' (with motivational interviewing), helping them develop pro-social support, and offering continuing consolidation of skills and plans during any transition and times of change (via a programme called the New Me MOT)

They will be asked to repeat good practices, reflect on them and look at what is happening in the here and now, rather than what they expect to happen.

There should be problem-solving training, to include, insight and awareness Sex education, emotional management and using positive personal rules.

The treatment uses positive inter-personal communication, good social support networks and peers mentoring.

The men are encouraged to practice skills and fill in a "Life Map" to show what they have achieved in each area.

For more information on Kaizen contact **www.joechapman.co.uk**

Transfers

Transfers happen for a whole host of reasons some of them are planned and you will be aware they are due to happen, some you request and others just happen and you won't find out until moving day.

We will cover a few common reasons for a transfer but it is another thing that you just have to take on the chin and accept that they happen, you can't change it by kicking off, so you might as well embrace it.

If your prison categorisation changes, in other words, your risk level changes you are likely to be moved. If you are in a Cat C prison and you are always fighting, it is to be expected that you will be deemed a higher risk and moved to a Cat B prison.

The same can be said if you are well behaved, you engage with the regime and you have demonstrated that you are lower risk, then you will find yourself going to a Cat D prison.

As you approach your release date the prison may also try to move you closer to the area you will be released to. This may happen by a series of mini moves if where you are going is a long way away. So, you may be housed temporarily at another prison whilst another bus is arranged.

For some transfers, they are planned well in advance, for security reasons you are unlikely to ever be given an exact date and time but you may be afforded the luxury of knowing a move is coming.

The more likely scenario though is being told to pack on the day of the move.

A transfer doesn't just happen when you are moving to prison, the prison can, without warning, move you to a new cell or wing. Again, don't expect an eviction notice and 28 days to mentally prepare, you will be told on the day and given half an hour to pack.

If you are lucky you might get a trolley to pack on to but expect to be carrying the plastic bags to wherever you happen to be going.

The process for transferring you to another prison is kind of like the process that brought you to prison in reverse.

You will be checked out, your property will be checked and signed over to transport, if you have "borrowed" or acquired anything that wasn't on your prop card, you will lose it here.

You might get searched, speaking from experience though that tends to happen on the other side.

Once the necessary paperwork and checks are completed you will be reunited with your old sweaty nemesis, the sweatbox, so make sure you have used the toilet before you leave.

This journey isn't nearly as bad as the first one you took in these; the fear and anxiety will likely rear its head at some point because it is a new prison to get used to but nothing as bad as that journey from the court.

Once you arrive at the new establishment, you will have the pleasure of going through the checking in process all over again.

It will be up to the prison if you are searched again and it will be up to the prison what property you can have in your possession, they will even decide if your IEP status remains as it was or if you have to "earn" it from scratch.

Your phone credit, pin and canteen spends will follow you but if you had canteen ordered at your previous prison and this was uncollected, the funds will eventually be returned to you but you may have to wait to be able to order canteen in the new place.

"Resettlement" jails

Typically, these are what Cat D prisons are now referred to, the idea/claim is that this is where you come to start your reintegration into society.

Before we go off on a big rant about what they don't offer and why they are not what they claim to be we will explain what they are useful for.

If you are on a shorter sentence (of around 4 years and under) then they are a welcome change from closed conditions, as they offer a more relaxed regime - as their open prison status would suggest.

So, for those people who haven't done a long sentence or their crime isn't deemed high risk this is where you want to be.

There is still a regime to follow, you will still have to work or be in education, there are still rules to follow and you are still a prisoner.

But what you will get is a key to your cell, the ability to move around your housing block freely (providing you are in your block you can leave your "cell" whenever you like) but you will need to answer roll calls and when officers check during the night you will need to be in your room or the block.

You still order meals on a weekly menu list but the servery is generally more relaxed, the portions are a little bigger and you normally eat in a communal dining hall where you collect meals from.

So, when you compare that to closed prison, open prison wins hands down every time.

But, and there is always a but, prison authorities insist on calling them "resettlement" prisons so, it is not unreasonable to expect them to do some resettling.

What they have become, is what much of the justice system has become; tick-box exercises that do nothing but show an audit trail of people seen.

They do not house people, they can't because they ended most contracts with housing providers when they brought in the epic failure that was the CRC.

They often fail to get the people out to work that requires it, the people they do send out end up having their money taxed by the prison so they can't build up their rent deposits and the work offered is often manual and eliminates older or educated prisoners from wanting or being able to do it.

Open prisons could offer so much more but they simply fail to understand even the most basic needs and challenges prisoners face on release.

Terry met a guy called Ali in HMP Springhill, he had served 18 years at the time and was getting ready for release in the next couple of years.

Ali went to prison before smartphones and before everything had gone online to the extent it is today.

His first-day release from the prison ended and he returned to speak to Terry.

Expecting a story of joy and excitement, Terry was shocked and taken back by what he heard.

"To be honest Tel, I think I would be better off attacking a guard and failing my probation hearing.

I'm not ready for going out, everything uses computers, I went to the bank and instead of people there was a machine - how do you talk to that?

I went to the jobcentre too, I wanted to look at job boards - there weren't any, just computer screens"

This is not an uncommon problem for long term prisoners. Resettlement prisons should be teaching them to get used to a very different world but they are not.

Terry asked the Governor why the jobcentre and banks couldn't set up fake computers in the prison for older guys to practice on and he was told it was a ridiculous suggestion that wasn't needed.

The world has moved on and it is taken for granted that people will just move on with it, but there are very basic, fundamental skills that prisons should be equipping people with and they don't.

This is another example of people without lived experience making decisions and assuming the knowledge level of people without actually asking.

HMP Springhill like many open prisons fails in its role as a resettlement establishment.

Probation

You will likely have heard of probation already and as we explain in the CRC section it has now been split into two entities - National Probation Service (NPS) and CRC's.

The NPS look after the higher risk offenders and are still publicly owned rather than privatised.

That being said, like most of the justice system it is extremely underfunded and its ability to help offenders has been significantly reduced over the many years of budget cuts.

Probation are a crucial part of you remaining out of prison, you will need to attend regular meetings with your officer following your release and they can start the process of recall to prison if you fail to adhere to your license conditions.

If you are unaware of how prison sentences work, then the vast majority will only serve a certain amount of time inside a prison, a 4-year prison sentence for example will consist of 2 years in prison and then 2 years monitored in the community.

Therefore, probation and community resettlement companies become an important part of your life outside of custody.

Terry's favourite topic - CRC's

What you will be told the CRC's do and what the reality of CRC's are, are two completely different things.

Let us first start with what the CRC's are supposed to do and how they came to be part of the prison system.

In 2015 the fatal decision was taken to break the probation service in two, one was to look after more serious offenders and would be kept in public ownership. The other half would be community-based monitoring for lower-risk offenders but crucially this would be privatised and contracted out.

The role the CRC's were to take, was to deal with reintegrating prisoners into society, the role the probation service used to fill.

Formerly, the probation service worked with other departments and was able to offer housing, links to jobs, links to health and social care and had more power to get you on to courses.

This is what the CRC's promised and they were to be paid an extortionate amount to provide this.

The problem with having a private business run a service like this is they are profit-making entities that are bound to their shareholders and for that reason, they will never have the true interests of the offender at heart.

The CRC's claim that they are a through the gate service that encompasses all of the key pillars of rehabilitation - education, housing, family ties, employment, debt/financial help and

From my own experience of CRC's at HMP Springhill I can tell you that they are inadequate, they are paid for a 12-week contract (in the prison environment) with each service user. This contract is paid not on results but on the application form you fill out, so they are paid by audit and not results, which is a major flaw in the contract as there is no incentive to deliver.

What the contract means is that when you enter the 12-weeks before the release date, you will meet with the CRC (unless you fall under the National Probation Service).

12 weeks is not an adequate amount of time to resolve anything but the most damning part of this service is that they cannot refer you directly anywhere, they can merely signpost you to other services (that are also just signposting) - when we say signposting what we mean is this, they can tell you company x might have housing available, but they can't book you an appointment, they can't influence a decision, all they can do is tell you the company exists.

Terry, for example, told HMP Springhill on arrival (some 12 months before his release date) that he would be homeless on release and that he needed either work to earn a rent deposit or complex assistance with housing.

Knowing how the prison system works, Terry immediately pursued the CRC because he knew that his need was greater than the 12 weeks they normally operated on.

He was told by the CRC on several occasions that their 92% success rate in housing prisoners was proof that their service was efficient and not to worry.

Terry did worry because housing is essential in maintaining a life outside of crime.

Terry spoke to the CRC at least once a week for his entire sentence - he left homeless.

This is fully documented and evidenced in his upcoming book - The final countdown to my freedom (available on amazon and kindle).

Terry would go on to learn that the 92% success rate the CRC would champion for their success was another example of dishonest data manipulation that has become systemic throughout the prison system.

A clear example of this is that on the day of your release you are required to provide an address and postcode of where you will be living, as this is dependent on you getting a travel warrant.

Terry told reception that he had no address as he had been failed by their support services (the CRC), he was then asked to give an address and that any address would suffice because they did not have a system in place to issue travel warrants where there is no fixed abode.

On the day of your release, most men will have no money for leaving prison (apart from their discharge grant) and will then give any address to be able to travel to the towns and cities that they consider home.

By giving any address, you are wrongly classing yourself as a housing success because in the eyes of the prison authorities you have indicated that you have somewhere to go and live, which is their intention.

This is the way they manipulate the data.

Terry refused to give an address because he didn't have one and he forms part of 8% of the official data says the system failed - he left with his discharge grant, a bag and a tent.

This was after being told by the serving governor at the time, that HMP Grendon and Springhill was the Rolls Royce of housing ex-offenders.

We document this here, not to worry you but to highlight the fact that you should not rely on these services to help you and to give you ample warning so that you can decide as early as possible to avoid one of the biggest pitfalls in your rehabilitation.

Pursuing housing will still prove difficult as you will struggle to prove that you have lived somewhere long enough to qualify for council housing and the fact that no one will reserve accommodation for your intended release date makes the task even harder.

Our advice is to ensure that you have friends or family that you can stay with whilst you sort the issue out on release.

To better reflect the true picture of what is happening to prisoners on release and to hopefully shine a light on the bigger picture, we would encourage everyone who does not have a permanent fixed address to call their own, to say you are being released as no fixed abode and help stop this intentional manipulation of data.

Now, we understand that you may have read that and thought why bother with the CRC at all - well post-release if you do not fall under the National Probation Service (NPS) then you will have to take part in their form-filling exercise or face going back to prison.

When the contract was privatised the CRC took over the community monitoring of offenders so you will have to visit them in the community.

They will also monitor your tag if you have one (HTC) and make sure that you are staying out of trouble.

The reality again is that they have no power of referral in the community so apart from inconveniencing you once a week (then once a fortnight and finally once a month as you progress and become more trusted) they really can't help you.

A friend of ours, Richard was placed in a BASS hostel on his release for 3 months on a tag - he told the CRC at the end of his 12 weeks BASS stay he would be homeless, they didn't help him.

He told his offender manager he was at risk of reoffending because of the situation and he got a voucher for a food bank and told if he reoffended he would be recalled to prison.

So, they are a necessary evil because they do have the power to get you recalled to prison which, let's face it having got through your sentence is probably not on your to-do list.

They are also another example of the UK Government throwing money away on service providers that provide no service.

ROTL (Release on Temporary License)

As you get towards the end of your sentence you will qualify for ROTL it is a license that grants you temporary release from prison.

Earlier in your sentence, if you need to leave the prison for a funeral or something important, you may be granted an assisted release but you will be chained to an officer the whole time.

Typically, ROTL's come when you get to Cat D prisons and you will need to qualify for the prison specific terms and be risk assessed.

ROTL allows you to be released from the prison either for the day or overnight, there will be strict rules attached to the license and you will have to give a detailed plan on what and where you plan to go and do.

Cat D prisons also offer community work and some even have paid jobs that you can apply to go out for (the prison will take a big chunk of that around 40%) - these require a license to allow you out.

Failure to follow the rules and guidelines on these licenses will result in future ROTL being cancelled.

It is very much a way for the prison service to test your suitability for permanent release, this is particularly true of longer-term prisoners who need to satisfy a parole board before release.

Relationships on release

A strange thing for us to speak about perhaps but the reality is that things will have changed for you and your partner by the time you come out of prison.

If you are lucky to have had someone stand by you whilst you served your sentence then this information is particularly relevant to you.

Being in prison your life will feel like it has stood still, you will expect to leave and everything will be the same as before. It won't.

Life on the outside has carried on, your partner has adjusted to you not being around and got on with life dealing with everything that has been thrown their way.

This is important because if you did nothing around the house before going to prison then your partner has got used to not tidying up and running around after you.

If you had certain jobs before you went to prison, like reading the kids bedtime story, don't be surprised if they have got used to and prefer your partner doing it.

Life carried on without you and you will have to fit into the new way of doing things, otherwise, your relationship will struggle.

There may also be resentment from your partner that you were not around, this is something else you are going to have to accept because they, whether you like it or not, held the fort down whilst you were away.

Our opinion of the Justice system

Rather than this just being a book of procedure and rules we also felt it prudent to provide you with an overview of our thoughts about what is broken with the justice system and how it could be improved.

For us prison shouldn't simply be about punishment, prison should be societies opportunity to put right the things in someone's life that lead to crime.

We aren't talking about some utopia where crime doesn't exist and prisons aren't needed, of course, there will always be a need for them to exist, we are talking about real change in the way in which "punishment" is viewed and escaping the flawed logic that more time equals less crime.

Harsher sentences with the idea they act as a deterrent are absurd, you only have to look at countries where there is still the death penalty and some of the longest prison sentences on the planet - crime still exists and in some cases is higher than other comparable countries.

The U.S, for example, has murder rates that are higher in states that carry the death penalty than those without, we aren't talking about one or two murders per state, in some states, they are as much as 101% above the national average.

We could produce stats and numbers to evidence any argument, the fact is numbers can be used or distorted to prove or disprove any argument so we won't get bogged down with them.

What we can do though is highlight the fact that any justice system that wishes to be effective in the reduction of crime must understand the reasons for crime.

Understanding crime and the causes of it is half the battle because often investigators and then judges don't wish to explore this.

Poverty or homelessness is not an excuse to break the law and we are not arguing that that is the case. But, homelessness leads to crime for several reasons and the resources it takes to put someone in prison could easily be used to address the problem a different way.

Typically, it costs around £120,000 to put someone in prison, it then costs approximately £35,000 a year to keep them there.

Our argument would be that community-based housing, education and support would be significantly cheaper than incarceration.

We completely understand the common argument we hear when we raise this "that is rewarding criminality", you wouldn't just get a house, there would be community work built into the new style of sentence and it would be work that would beneficial to local councils that could potentially lead to paid work.

One of the biggest problems with the justice system, in our opinion, is that we have had successive Governments where their focus is on short-termism rather than a planned, well thought out, structured long-term vision.

Prisons will always be needed however the longer sentence brigade are simply advocating for a bigger prison bill and not addressing crime and the causes of crime.

There are many examples around the world with much more successful systems than the UK, such as; Denmark, Iceland, Netherlands, South Korea, Japan - they have very different approaches to criminals which revolve around community and education rather than simply punitive measures.

Some former prisoners have become apologists for our system who claim that culturally the UK could never have a functioning system like that and it works.

The simple fact is that it has never been properly tried and until we attempt a newer, modern, more encompassing approach to crime that argument simply doesn't fly.

Real change for our justice system is achievable but it needs to begin with the social and economic factors that contribute towards crime.

Courts and Legal Aid

The first critical point we need to make is that cuts over the last ten to fifteen years by successive Governments have crippled the system right the way through.

What that means is that from the police trying to enforce the law to the probation service and community services trying to keep people on the straight and narrow there is a real lack of funding to run effective services.

So, some crimes should be brought to court that never get there because the police are unable to investigate them fully and some people fall through the gaps because support services are not in place to help them.

The numbers back up what we are saying - in 2019 the number of people dealt with by the courts fell to its lowest level since records began and this isn't because there is less crime.

Knife crime is at its highest level since 2011, fraud offences are up 15% and robbery was up 11%.

The Ministry of Justice funding had fallen by 26% in real terms since 2010 and those cuts are having a profound impact.

The current estimate is that only 8% of crime results in a conviction, which means that 92% of crimes currently go unpunished.

What you have as result in the courts is a huge backlog of cases, fewer cases being heard and fewer courtrooms open to hear them.

Pre covid-19 the courts were reporting that almost 40,000 cases were waiting to be heard.

We suppose that this all is good practice for if you end up going to prison because it gets you used to waiting.

The court that hears your trial should be relative to the location where that crime was committed but this can change and sometimes at very short notice.

An example of this is one guy who lived in Liverpool, who was accused of a crime in Basingstoke, which was listed for trial in Winchester and it got moved when Winchester couldn't hear it to Portsmouth.

Having already made sure he was in Winchester, he had no means of getting to Portsmouth the next day and his none attendance went against him.

We don't know the answer to this because the courts need to hear cases when they can hear them, but there needs to be some consideration for where the accused lives in relation to the court because this would reduce no shows and the subsequent warrants issued for their arrest.

It is not unusual in the current climate for you to have to wait anywhere up to 18 months for your trial to start, even if you are listed to be heard for trial, if something happens with an overrunning trial before you, your case may be adjourned several times.

There was an example of a serious assault where an eyewitness saw the two men that committed the crime. The trial was scheduled and subsequently adjourned 3 times, the witness lived in Dubai and had to fly over each time at his own expense.

By the time the fourth trial date came, he was unable or unwilling to spend money to travel again and the case collapsed without an eye witness, meaning the people that carried out a brutal attack were free to walk away.

And then we move to legal aid. Legal funding has fallen by 31% between 2010 and 2018 and this seriously hinders someone's right to a fair trial because people are representing themselves in court because they simply cannot afford representation.

In 2016 18% of all cases heard had self-representation, in comparison, there was only 2% in 2010.

So, the odds are fully stacked against people before you even arrive at court.

The solution to this is fairly simple, everyone should be provided legal representation regardless of circumstance and the courts need to be funded properly to function correctly and in a timelier manner.

The police funding needs addressing too, currently, some people should be in prison, not in prison and due to the situation with legal aid, there are people in prison, who shouldn't be there because the system has failed them.

We are not saying the court system isn't flawed when it operates because it is, innocent people are found guilty and guilty people are found innocent all the time but the Governments underfunding, of what is an essential pillar in a functioning society is in itself a criminal act because people are being denied justice.

The court system in the UK is rumoured to be at the brink of collapse, the current UK Government's rhetoric of more prisons and longer sentences is just hot air if you don't have the police numbers you need to enforce the law and the court system to uphold the law.

Drug de-criminalisation - Time for a conversation?

We fully understand anyone reading this who has lost someone to drugs will have an immediate response of absolutely not, but the war on drugs is a fallacy it is not working and there needs to be a real discussion about a different approach.

The courts and the justice system are clogged up with drug users, the war on drugs has cost the US alone $51billion a year. Drug use in the U.S increases year on year.

The UK as mentioned has seen its police funding slashed since 2010 and the cost of enforcing current drug legislation is estimated at £16billion a year. Drug use in the UK increases year on year - the UK is one of the biggest cocaine consumers in Europe.

Prohibition doesn't work!

In 1920 the Volstead act came into force in America for 13 years, prohibition of alcohol was trialled and it was a disaster. You had illegal distilleries and homemade low-quality alcohol was rife.

It didn't prevent drinking, it simply opened the door for black market trade, in the long run, it did more damage than have regulated laws and legal suppliers.

There have been successes with de-criminalising drugs around the world, the key is de-criminalising and not legalising - de-criminalising drug use removes the stigma associated with drug use and the fear that seeking help could lead to a conviction.

By de-criminalising you also allow for safe spaces to open up, again we know that the gut reaction to that suggestion is that we are advocating legal crack dens.

In a way, I suppose we are but by having a controlled environment where help is on hand you are taking the strain off emergency services and removing the problem from squats, car parks and other areas in the community.

You also allow support services and drug workers to be on hand when someone decides they need to access help, along with practical services like needle exchange and safe disposal.

Portugal for example, de-criminalised all drugs in 2000/2001. they looked at the problem from a public health point of view and decided that instead of spending money on enforcing drug laws they would concentrate on building support networks for drug users.

Over the next 15 years, they significantly reduced drug use, their death rates fell, heroin use has reduced by over 50% and crime related to drugs fell significantly too.

The biggest testament to their success though is that since they took this measure no one from any political party is calling to return to their old drug laws.

A common misconception is that by taking this approach you suddenly open the flood gates for everyone to become a heroin addict - the data indicates that there is very little change in regular drug habits, so a heroin user will still be a heroin user, a non-heroin user will remain a non-heroin user.

What the research does show is that actually drug use tends to come from a lack of connection, boredom or an escape from something - the approach Portugal took was to address those gaps.

Legality has very little influence on drug use, what it does affect is whether someone will feel they can tell a doctor or a friend or a family member they have a problem.

Our stance is very much that a new approach needs to be looked at - drug use in the UK increases year on year - in 2018 for example drug-related deaths in the UK rose by 16% (4,359).

The problem isn't going away.

The prison system

We have touched on a lot of the issues with prisons already, properly funding would be a start but it has to be funded with a long-term goal in place - something that cannot be said there is, in the current system.

From your first night in prison, you are being set up to fail, in everything post-release that Terry has gone on to achieve, he has achieved it in spite of the system, not because of it and that is a problem.

The way prison induction is run allows abuse, by ensuring that you have no money to spend (even if you have funds available) leaves people open to being exploited to run up debts.

Whilst we can understand the need for prisoners to do certain jobs throughout the prison, the inductions are somewhere that we strongly disagree with prisoners being so involved.

The induction orderlies are low paid jobs, some are paid by other prisoners in the prison to extract information from new arrivals that can be used on the wings. For example, if someone is a heroin addict this information will get to the wings before a prisoner gets there and they will be targeted for sales.

It also allows orderlies to "lend" items to newcomers that don't know any better and thus saddling them with debt before they have even arrived on their first wing.

Debts in prison are behind a lot of the increasing violence, it is behind a lot of the drugs and it ultimately funds people to lead extremely lavish (by prison standards) lives in prison.

By making the induction process more inviting and ensuring that prisoners have access to one or two simple luxuries you remove the need for people to turn to fellow inmates.

Once you remove that need, you shut down the market available for the men that rely on saddling new inmates with new debts.

Extending the induction process so that you can fully understand the new inmates is another thing that could head off problems before they start. If someone is a known addict the induction process should highlight this and allow additional time to go cold turkey at the start of the sentence.

This approach would also require healthcare to not overprescribe drug replacements and work with the prison.

Whilst the approach of earned privileges is understandable, there should perhaps be a system in place for an external purchase (from friends or family) of a home comforts pack - a proper duvet, pillow, dressing gown, flip flops etc.

These are things that may assist those struggling to feel more at home and integrate them into the prison quicker - the upshot of doing this is the prison makes money on the pack regardless and there are potentially fewer problems with new arrivals.

Writing these things looks simple and I am sure you are reading this and thinking "Would a duvet make a difference?"

The short answer is yes, prison is hard to adjust to and some struggle more than others - when people are under stress they react differently to things.

In the last ten years, the prison service has lost roughly 10,000 officers from their total number, they haven't had to deal with fewer prisoners in that time.

This has a knock-on effect on the quality of job they can do, prisons are less safe than they were when there were 10,000 more officers. With fewer officers comes less time to deal with people one to one, it also means there is less time to deal with seemingly basic requests - when basic requests are not met it causes frustration and when you add frustration into an already difficult period of someone's life then you increase the chance of irrational responses and this is also feeding into the increase in violence.

Officer numbers are not just about x amount of staff, it is also about the quality of those staff. Prisons lost experienced staff, prison is complex and no matter how long your training course is, there is no substitute for time on the wings.

Experienced officers knew or know how to run wings effectively, they can see the people that need additional help, they sense trouble, they had earned their stripes and carry themselves differently which breeds respect. You can have hard ass newbies that demand respect and perhaps they get what they perceive to be respected but it is very very different.

There have been enough former inmates that have provided constructive information that the prison service could take on board but this is ignored, generally because people in authority would rather pay out millions to consultants who have "theories" about what will work.

Using these ex-prisoners who are willing to put suggestions out there is something other countries embrace, this could also be a viable employment option for ex-offenders who have shown a real determination and dedication to turn their lives around.

There is also an opportunity for prisons to categorise their prison within the prison, rewarding those who follow the rules and adhere to the regime and punishing those who want to waste their time.

If you had an internal policy of having, for example, 2 x A cat wings, 2 x B cat wings, 2 x C cat wings and finally 2 x D cat wings or whatever combination works.

Those on the A Cat wing run the risk of being shipped out to a lower cat prison with a stricter regime and those on the D cat wing could go to a more relaxed prison.

The regime on each wing would correspond to the amount of bang-up, gym etc. they are eligible for, they also qualify first for the better jobs and education available.

You reward the ones that wish to make more of their time in prison and punish the ones that simply want to mess around.

This will also impact sentence management for prisoners, if you are in a B cat prison but on an A cat wing then you cannot move to a C cat prison until your behaviour warrants being on the D cat wing.

A system like this would also prevent genuine troublemakers from making an open prison and allow the prison to focus on those making a genuine effort to improve their circumstances.

It is however the kind of progressive thinking that is lacking throughout the prison system, we offer it as a suggestion, perhaps it would never work but what we have found is that people are set in their ways and when you get a Governor that is willing to try something different they often end up with their hands tied by red tape and politics.

We then arrive at the prisons themselves, some are run down, most are overcrowded and all are underfunded.

Prisons will never be a vote winner for politicians, the British media has already painted the picture of UK prisons as holiday camps and generally whenever you talk about a prisoner to Joe Public, they imagine the worst possible crimes and talk about bringing back the death sentence as if that is some kind answer to crime.

In 1996 there was a theory floated called 'broken windows theory' by Wilson and Kelling, this (in a very basic summary) suggested that you would get more crime and disorder in run-down neighbourhoods than in better-maintained areas.

They proved it to be correct, although a later study in 2006 suggested there was no difference.

However, this is something that Terry witnessed first-hand during his sentence, the cockroach-infested HMP Pentonville was more volatile than the better-kept prisons.

He even admits that he gave less of a shit when the prison was a rundown mess than he did when the surroundings were well maintained.

This is a huge problem for the older prisons in the estate because they are in desperate need of modernisation but as mentioned earlier it will never be a vote winner so the problem will get worse year on year.

Final Thought

Prison doesn't have to be all doom and gloom, there are many things you will experience in prison that will help you become a better person if you are willing to take those lessons moving forward in your life.

You will have learnt compromise and patience.

You would have also learned one of the most important lessons we believe you can ever learn, you will have learned to manage boredom. This book was written initially during the 2020 global Covid-19 pandemic and every single ex-offender we have spoken to during the "lockdown" found it easy.

Adaptability is something else you perfect whilst in prison and this will be something you will rely on if you are to stay out of prison in the future.

The road into employment and staying away from crime isn't going to be easy, you will be punished long after the prison element of your sentence is over, typically 4 years after your initial sentence (for example, 2-year sentence - 1 year in prison then 1 year in the community followed by 4 years until the conviction is "spent").

In some cases, your conviction will never class as spent.

However, some companies can support you, at the back of this book is a list of helpful resources and support groups.

Our final thought on the criminal justice system:

"You can throw money at as many people in expensive suits, to design fancy courses that claim to fix the criminal mind as much as you like. If you continue to release men and women into the same environment and problems as they had before they committed a crime then you will end up with the same result.

Nothing changes, if nothing changes"

- THE END -

Useful Links

www.prisonadvice.org.uk

www.stgilestrust.org.uk

www.step-together.org.uk

www.clinks.org

www.gov.uk/support-for-families-friends-of-prisoners

www.prisonreformtrust.org.uk

www.prisonersfamilies.org

www.peoplefirstinfo.org.uk

www.nacro.org.uk

www.cleansheet.org.uk

www.russellwebster.com

www.prosper4jobs.co.uk

www.forwardtrust.org.uk

hub.unlock.org.uk

www.princes-trust.org.uk

caringforexoffenders.org

Printed in Great Britain
by Amazon